MARITIME HISTORY SERIES

Series Editor

John B. Hattendorf, *Naval War College*

Volumes Published in this Series

Pietro Martire d'Anghiera, et al.
The history of travayle in the West and East Indies (1577)
Introduction by Thomas R. Adams,
John Carter Brown Library

Willem Ysbrandsz. Bontekoe
Die vier und zwantzigste Schiffahrt (1648)
Introduction by Augustus J. Veenendaal, Jr.,
Instituut voor Nederlandse Geschiedenis, The Hague

Josiah Burchett
A complete history of the most remarkable transactions at sea (1720)
Introduction by John B. Hattendorf,
Naval War College

Alvise Cà da Mosto
Questa e una opera necessaria a tutti li naviga[n]ti (1490)
bound with:
Pietro Martire d'Anghiera
Libretto de tutta la navigatione de Re de Spagna (1504)
Introduction by Felipe Fernández-Armesto,
Oxford University

Martín Cortés
The arte of navigation (1561)
Introduction by D. W. Waters,
National Maritime Museum, Greenwich

John Davis
The seamans secrets (1633)
Introduction by A. N. Ryan,
University of Liverpool

Francisco Faleiro
Tratado del esphera y del arte del marear (1535)
Introduction by Timothy Coates,
College of Charleston

Gemma, Frisius
De principiis astronomiae & cosmographiae (1553)
Introduction by C. A. Davids,
University of Leiden

Tobias Gentleman
Englands way to win wealth, and to employ ships and marriners (1614)
bound with:
Robert Kayll
The trades increase (1615)
and
Dudley Digges
The defence of trade (1615)
and
Edward Sharpe
Britaines busse (1615)
Introduction by John B. Hattendorf,
Naval War College

William Hacke
A collection of original voyages (1699)
Introduction by Glyndwr Williams,
Queen Mary and Westfield College, University of London

*Marine architecture:
or Directions for carrying on a ship from the first laying of the keel
to her actual going to sea* (1739)
Introduction by Brian Lavery,
National Maritime Museum, Greenwich

Pedro de Medina
L'art de naviguer (1554)
Introduction by Carla Rahn Phillips,
University of Minnesota

Thomas Pownall
The administration of the colonies (4th ed., 1768)
Introduction by Daniel A. Baugh, Cornell University,
and Alison Gilbert Olson,
University of Maryland, College Park

*St. Barthélemy and the Swedish West India Company:
A selection of printed documents, 1784-1814*
Introduction by John B. Hattendorf,
Naval War College

John Seller
Practical navigation (1680)
Introduction by Michael Richey,
Royal Institute of Navigation

*Shipbuilding Timber for the British Navy:
Parliamentary papers, 1729-1792*
Introduction by R. J. B. Knight,
National Maritime Museum, Greenwich

Jean Taisnier
A very necessarie and profitable booke concerning navigation (1579?)
Introduction by John Parker,
James Ford Bell Library

Lodovico de Varthema
Die ritterlich un[d] lobwirdig Rayss (1515)
Introduction by George Winius,
University of Leiden

Gerrit de Veer
The true and perfect description of three voyages (1609)
Introduction by Stuart M. Frank, Kendall Whaling Museum

Isaak Vossius
A treatise concerning the motion of the seas and winds (1677)
together with
De motu marium et ventorum (1663)
Introduction by Margaret Deacon,
University of Southampton

Peter Carl Zimmermann
Reise nach Ost- und West-Indien (1771)
together with
Journaal van het Oost-Indische Schip Blydorp (1734)
and
*Rampspoedige Reys-Beschryving, ofte Journaal van 's Ed:
Oostindische Compagnies Schip Blydorp* (1735)
Introduction by Roelof van Gelder,
Amsterdam, The Netherlands

A very necessarie and profitable booke concerning navigation
(1579?)

by Joannes Taisnier

Translated by Richard Eden

Reproduced in facsimile
with an Introduction by
JOHN PARKER

```
WITHDRAWN
SEP 2 0 2023
John Carter Brown Library
```

Published for the
JOHN CARTER BROWN LIBRARY
by
SCHOLARS' FACSIMILES & REPRINTS
DELMAR, NEW YORK
1999

SCHOLARS' FACSIMILES & REPRINTS
ISSN 0161–7729
SERIES ESTABLISHED 1936
VOLUME 480

First Printing 1999

Published by Scholars' Facsimiles & Reprints
Delmar, New York 12054-0344, U.S.A.

New matter in this edition
© 1999 Academic Resources Corporation
All rights reserved

Printed and made in the United States of America

The publication of this work was assisted by a grant from
The National Endowment for the Humanities

This book
is reproduced from a copy in the John Carter Brown Library
at Brown University, Providence, Rhode Island.

∞ The paper used in this publication conforms to the
American National Standard for Information Sciences—
Permanence of Paper for Publications and Documents
in Libraries and Archives ANSI/NISO/Z39.48—1992.

Library of Congress Cataloging-in-Publication Data

Taisnier, Jean, 1508–ca. 1562.

A very necessarie and profitable booke concerning navigation (1579?) /
by Joannes Taisnier ; translated by Richard Eden ;
reproduced in facsimile with an introduction by John Parker.
      p.   cm. —
(Maritime history series)
(Scholars' Facsimiles & Reprints, ISSN 0161-7729 ; v. 480)
Originally published: London : Richard Jugge, 1579?
ISBN 0-8201-1480-4 (alk. paper)
1. Navigation—Early works to 1800.
I. Title. II. Series.
III. Series: Maritime history series (Delmar, N.Y.)
     VK551.T27   1999
  623.89—dc21   99-10374
                       CIP

Introduction

Richard Eden's translation of *Opusculum Perpetua Memoria dignissimum* . . ., a collection of scientific treatises gathered by Joannes Taisnier, and its publication under the title *A very necessarie and profitable booke concerning navigation,* is a reflection of Eden's passion for bringing England into the Age of Discovery and the scramble for overseas empire.[1] His choice of this text reveals the lack of clarity in his mind as to the division of knowledge between science, pseudoscience, superstition, and tradition. In that, Eden was a man of his time. England's foremost scientist in the sixteenth century was John Dee, who was at the same time a magician, a cabalist, and, some claimed, a sorcerer.[2]

There was much in addition to science that needed to be defined in England in Eden's time. The nation as a united political entity dated from the first Tudor, Henry VII, whose reign began in 1485. The nation's religion was in the process of definition and the outcome was far from certain. The idea of empire was yet to be discussed widely, and the intellectual tools requisite to the discussion were almost totally lacking at mid-century when Eden began his career as translator-editor and advocate of overseas empire. His choice of Taisnier's book for translation was his final effort to bring to English readers the type of scientific information necessary to an expansionist future.

In placing this work in its historical and intellectual context, it is well to consider that at mid-sixteenth century no published text in the English language described the voyages of Columbus, Vespucci, Magellan, or Cartier. Nor were there accounts of Spanish conquest in the New World, or of Portuguese enterprise in India. Eden began the process of bringing

---

1. The full title and imprint of Taisnier's book are as follows: *Omnia Perpetus Memoria Dignissimum, De Natura Magnetis, et Eius Effectibus. Item De Motu Continuo. Demonstratio Proportionum Motuum Localium, Contra Aristotelem & Alios Philosophos. De Motu Alio Celerrimo, Hactenus Incognito* (Coloniae: Apud Joannem Birckmannum, M.D.LXII).

2. Peter J. French, *John Dee: The World of an Elizabethan Magus* (London: Routledge & Kegan Paul, 1972) presents a good picture of the scientific milieu of sixteenth-century England.

English readers into the Age of Discovery with a small book, *A Treatyse of the Newe India* (1533), a collection of pieces of geographical and exploration information gathered from Sebastian Münster's *Cosmographia* (Basel, 1544).[3] He expanded his scope greatly in 1555 with his *Decades of the Newe Worlde or West India*, a translation of Pietro Martire d'Anghiera's *Decadas* of 1516, with additional material from the writings of Oviedo, López de Gómara, Vespucci, and others, including Vanuccio Biringucci, whose ideas about gold were of particular interest to Eden.[4] His next empire-promoting project was a translation in 1561 of the *Arte de Navegar* by Martín Cortés, one of the two leading navigation texts of its time.[5] It was destined to have great popularity in England, with nine editions in English by 1630. It was in the 1579 edition that the companion work, the translation of Taisnier's collection, was announced.

Eden came to the view that his duty to his country should be that of translator and editor of maritime and expansionist literature from a background both academic and commercial. Born about 1520 into a family involved in the wool trade with Europe, he enrolled as a student at Cambridge in 1534. The University was at that time taking its first steps toward integrating mathematics and science into the curriculum, due in part to the influence of Erasmus, and Eden's tutor was Thomas Smith, prominent among English mathematicians of the time. Eden probably acquired some of his knowledge of languages at Cambridge also. Another prominent thread in England's intellectual fabric during Eden's lifetime was antiquarianism, which sought to find in England's past

---

3. The text of this work is included in Edward Arber, ed., *The First Three English Books on America* (Westminster: Archibald Constable, 1895; rpt. New York: Kraus Reprints, 1971); a facsimile edition was issued by University Microfilms (Ann Arbor, 1966).

4. See the facsimile of the revised second edition of this work, published in this series, under the title *The History of Travayle in the West and East Indies* (1577), with an introduction by Thomas R. Adams.

5. Eden's translation was from Martín Cortés, *Breve Compendio de la Sphere y de la Arte de Navegar* (Seville: Anton Allvarez, 1551). A facsimile edition was published in Zaragoza by the Institucion Fernando el Catolico, 1945, and in this series in 1992, with an introduction by D. W. Waters. The other major navigation text of the time was Pedro de Medina, *Arte de Navegar* (Valladolid: F. Fernandez de Cordua, 1545), of which a facsimile of the French edition of 1554 appears in this series with an introduction by Carla Rahn Phillips.

Introduction

historic justification for a glorious future. The legendary King Arthur provided such a model, but in Eden's view bringing the future to flower required the efforts of Englishmen now—all who had talents to give. He wrote, "In certayne small and obscure members of the commonwealth, consisteth no small increase to the perfection of the whole."[6]

Armed with this conviction, and with considerable talent as a translator and scientist, Eden set about a career of discerning useful ideas, attempting to sort out truth from belief, science from myth and magic. He was not without experience in this type of sorting at a fundamental level, for he was involved in an attempt to create gold in a laboratory and was fined for his efforts.

After the publication of his *The Arte of Navigation* in 1561, Eden went off to France to serve as deputy to the bishop of Chartres. What his duties were we do not know, but the ten years he spent abroad must have been for him a rich time of meeting scholars and finding books by authors little known in England. He wrote in his introduction to the Taisnier text that he found "these bookes here followyng printed, whiche I brought with me out of Fraunce."

Among the people he knew in France was Jacques Besson, professor of mathematics at Orléans, in whom Eden saw the soul of Archimedes revived, and whose book *Instrumentorum et Machinarum* (Orléans, 1569) he refers to as "conteyning the fourmes and portractes of syxtie engines of marveylous strange and profytable device," some of which he described in detail, along with other machines he had seen or learned of during his time in Europe. Clearly he was fascinated by the science and technology of his day, and if somewhat gullible, not completely so, for he questions his friend Sebastian Cabot's claim on his deathbed that he had, by "divine revelation," knowledge of the means to determine longitude at sea. Eden writes, "but I thinke the good olde man, in that extreme age somewhat doted." But if not always a believer, he continued to be a searcher of modern science for answers to complex problems. He quoted Jean Fernel, a French scholar, on other means of knowing the longitude. He quoted at length a letter from Angelus Policianus (Johann

---

6. The most complete source of biographical information on Richard Eden is David Gwyn, "Richard Eden, Cosmographer and Alchemist," *Sixteenth Century Journal* 15:1 (1984): 13–34; for a commentary on Eden's life and works see John Parker, *Richard Eden, Advocate of Empire*, James Ford Bell Lecture no. 29 (Minneapolis, 1991). The quotation is from the first page of Eden's dedication in the 1561 edition of *The Arte of Navigation*.

Engel, 1463–1512) to Franciscus Casa concerning a device for tracking the motion of planets, and noted in Leonardo Fioravanti's *Specchio di Scientica Universale* (Venice, 1564) the description of a ship "which cannot peryshe eyther on the sea, or the lande." He suspects the author is claiming too much for his invention, adding "as for the moste parte is the maner of Italian writers." While absolving himself of belief, Eden goes on to describe Fioravanti's ship.

Yet for all his awareness of emerging scientific thought and its application to new inventions, Eden was ever aware of the classical authorities, frequently citing them, and when he considered the origins of navigation he went back to Noah and his ark.

In view of Eden's breadth of interest and knowledge, which is apparent in the dedication of this book to Sir William Winter, master of ordnance and surveyor of royal fleet, his choice of Taisnier's work as a subject for translation seems quite in order. Taisnier too was a man of many interests, enjoying a wide reputation throughout Europe's scholarly community. That reputation was not fully deserved, for much of what Taisnier wrote was derived from others rather than original work of his own. Eden gives no indication that he had met Taisnier, but his familiarity with Taisnier's work and reputation would have been natural due to the convergence of their interests.

Taisnier was born in Hainault in 1509 and his early education prepared him for an ecclesiastical career. He became tutor to the children of Charles V and accompanied him on his expedition to Tunis in 1533. He also went with the emperor to Italy. Thus began a broad experience of travel that introduced him to the world of scholarship. At various times he appears to have taught at the universities of Rome, Ferrara, Padua, Florence, and Palermo. He was for a time head of a school at Lessines in Hainault. He was director of musicians for Cardinal Francesco de Mendoza. In addition to his scientific studies he taught music and ancient and modern languages at various places. In 1558 he moved to Cologne where he served as master of the archepiscopal chapel. Between 1550 and 1562 he published at least six books, the texts of which were largely derived from earlier works dealing primarily with mathematics, astronomy, and astrology.[7]

---

7. Lynn Thorndike, *A History of Magic and Experimental Science during the First Thirteen Centuries of Our Era*, 8 vols. (New York: Columbia University Press, 1923-58), 5:280-89.

Introduction 13

Taisnier was known as an expert in chiromancy (the examination of human hands), which he related closely to astrology. He was indeed an excellent example of the conflation of science and magic in that era, and he plagiarized in both fields with impartiality. He is remembered primarily for his plagiarism of the treatise on the lodestone by Petrus Peregrinus of Maricourt, a thirteenth-century scholarly contemporary of Roger Bacon, and that plagiarism is included in this work which Eden selected for translation.

In his dedication to William Winter, Eden informs us that the translation came about when he returned from his sojourn in France, in 1573 or 1574, and met with Richard Jugge, the publisher of *The Arte of Navigation*. They discussed publishing a new edition, and Jugge made as a condition the translation of some other work on navigation which would be issued as a companion piece.[8] Eden chose Taisnier's work, although it is by no means primarily a navigation text comparable to his translation of Cortés. Nevertheless, it was touted on the title page of the 1579 edition of *The Arte of Navigation*: "Whereunto may be added at the wyl of the buyer, another very fruitful and necessary booke of Navigation." Eden's translation of Taisnier's work is undated, and the side note in the dedication which contains the date 1584 has caused some confusion. This is the note referred to above in which Johann Engel's letter to Franciscus Casa is described. The date is surely a misprint for 1484, for Engel died in 1512. He was active in the 1480s, having published an almanac and two books in that decade.[9] Eden died in 1575, and Richard Jugge in 1577. He was succeeded by his son John who died in 1578 or early 1579.[10] Nevertheless, both works carry the imprint of Richard Jugge, and since *The Arte of Navigation* is dated 1579, it seems reasonable to assume that the Taisnier work was published at the same time, both having been prepared by Richard Jugge.

In this work as in his other translations Eden limits his editorial intervention, reproducing the text without much editorial comment, although in this instance he does rearrange the sections dealing with

---

8. First page of dedication to Eden's translation.

9. The almanack was for the year 1484, published in Bamberg by Johann Sensenschmidt, 1483; the books were *Astrolabium Planum in Tabulis Ascendens* (Augsburg: Erhard Retdolt, 1488) and *Albumazaris de Magnis Conjunctionibus* (Augsburg: Erhard Retdolt, 1489).

10. *Dictionary of National Biography*, 10:1111–1112.

separate topics, as will be noted. He includes Taisnier's dedication to the archbishop of Cologne, in which Taisnier comments on the negative criticism that often befalls writers on mathematics and related subjects. The first part of the text is titled "Of the nature and effectes of the Lode stone, called in Latine Magnus." This has long been recognized as a plagiarism of the *Epistola de Magnete* of Petrus Peregrinus of Maricourt, written in the thirteenth century and first printed in Augsburg in 1558.[11] It begins by identifying various kinds of lodestones, the places where they are found, and the virtues of the lodestone, notably its polarity. Peregrinus believed the polarity of the stone was not due to the magnetism of the earth, but that it was from a celestial polarity. The magnetized needle and its utility as a mariner's compass was known, but probably not widely so, before Peregrinus, and he provides instruction for constructing a compass. He goes beyond that utility, however, for in finding the magnetic force in the celestial pole he believed that if a globular magnet were mounted so that its poles were tilted at an angle to the celestial pole, the constant turning of the celestial pole would keep the magnet in a state of constant motion. He alludes to the long search by philosophers of the past for continual motion, and he believed that with the lodestone he had at last found it. He describes the construction of a machine to capture this force and make it useful.

In the next part of the work, Eden transposes the third part of Taisnier's text to make it the second part, probably because of its significance for navigation. He titles it, "Of most swift motion by arte of Navigation." Here Taisnier deals with variations in the speed of ships, even those designed by the same shipwright and carrying similar cargo. He cites examples of voyages made in an incredibly short time which he had himself witnessed, so it is possible that this is a work of his own composition. It is a treatise on hull design, with rules of proportion by which the length to breadth ratio must be six to one, and the length to depth ratio ten to one. The use of light timber for construction and tallow applied to the ship's bottom complete the instructions, to which others could add improvements, "for in all sciences it is easyer to adde to inventions, then to invent." From this Taisnier goes on to describe a cauldron for descending under water in a space with trapped air,

---

11. Petrus Peregrinus, of Maricourt, *De Magnete, seu Rota Perpetui Motus, ibellus* (Augsburg: Achilles P. Gasser, 1558).

Introduction 15

observations on earthquakes at sea, distilling saltwater through wax, and other items of maritime interest.

In the original text, Taisnier carries this maritime theme forward with a long discussion of tides and their causes. In the translation Eden makes this a separate section, "Of the Flowing, and Reflowing, (that is) increase and decrease of the Sea, with the causes thereof, more exactly then hytherto hath been declared by any." This claim may be justified in that Taisnier brought into the causes of tides the effects of the sun. Taisnier identified Fredericus Delphinus, a professor of mathematics at Padua, as one of his sources. His others he identified merely as "divers learned men," while he claims some of the work as "partly by mine owne industrie," in Eden's words.[12] In addition to the moon and the sun, Taisnier also adds major planets among the forces affecting tides. In doing so he creates an elaborate celestial structure of points of strength and weakness through which the sun and moon pass to account for the regularity of high and low water, and in all of it the activating force is the light emanating from the sun, moon, and planets. A contemporary work, William Bourne's *A Regiment for the Sea* (1574, and many subsequent editions) presented a much more useful explanation of tides, as did Eden's *Arte of Navigation,* although these did not bring the sun into the calculation.[13]

In Taisnier's original work he included a section on local motion, following his work on continual motion. Eden made this the fourth section of his translation, titling it "Demonstration of properties of Motions Locall," and noting that it would be of more interest to learned philosophers than to mariners. This is Taisnier's confutation of Aristotle, which arose out of a lecture he presented in Rome where his reasoning had been challenged and he responded with argument and demonstration in the presence of many learned people. The issue was whether bodies of greater weight fell to earth more rapidly than materials of lesser weight. Taisnier cites no experiment to prove his point, but works it out mathematically, proving wrong Aristotle's view that heavier objects would fall more rapidly. Taisnier's theory originated with Giovanni

---

12. Federico Delphino, *De Fluxu et Refluxu Aquae Maruis* (Venice: Academia Veneta, 1559).

13. William Bourne, *A Regiment for the Sea and Other Writings on Navigation,* ed. E. G. R. Taylor (Cambridge University Press for the Hakluyt Society, series II, vol. XXXI, 1963).

Battista Benedetti, a Venetian mathematician who lectured at Rome, Parma, and Turin during the time that Taisnier was in Italy.[14]

Clearly, as Eden had noted, this was not a subject of particular interest to seamen, but Taisnier's scope of inquiry did not have marine subjects as a primary focus as Eden's did. Yet both men exemplified European scientific inquiry in the mid-sixteenth century. Taisnier was much more interested in theoretical studies than Eden, who sought to put his knowledge to practical use. Taisnier had a predilection for astrology, which Eden despised, having separated it out from astronomy. Eden had a mission for his work, preparing England for a part in the competition for overseas trade and empire. Taisnier had no such national attachment, and the force that drove him appears to have been self-glorification, along with a general spirit of inquiry typical of the intellectual spirit of his time.

JOHN PARKER
Curator Emeritus
James Ford Bell Library
Minneapolis, Minnesota

---

14. Benedetti first set forth his theory in the letter of dedication to his *Resolutio Omnium Euclidis Problematum* (Venice: Bartholomaeum Caesanum, 1553).

SUGGESTIONS FOR FURTHER READING

Arber, Edward, ed. *The First Three English Books on America.* Westminster, 1895. Rpt. New York, 1971.

Bourne, William. *A Regiment for the Sea.* Edited by E. G. R. Taylor. Cambridge, 1963.

French, Peter J. *John Dee: The World of an Elizabethan Magus.* London, 1972.

Goldstein, Thomas. *Dawn of Modern Science.* Boston, 1980.

Hall, A. Rupert. *The Scientific Revolution, 1500–1800.* London, 1954.

Johnson, Francis R. *Astronomical Thought in Renaissance England.* Baltimore, 1937.

Levy, F. J. *Tudor Historical Thought.* San Marino, 1967.

Medina, Pedro de. *A Navigator's Universe: The Libro de Cosmographia of 1538.* Edited by Ursula Lamb. Chicago, 1972.

Penrose, Boies. *Travel and Discovery in the Renaissance, 1420–1620.* Cambridge, Mass., 1952.

Taylor, E. G. R. *The Haven-Finding Art: A History of Navigation from Odysseus to Captain Cook.* London, 1956.

——————. *The Mathematical Practitioners of Tudor and Stuart England.* London, 1934.

Thorndike, Lynn. *A History of Magic and Experimental Science during the First Thirteen Centuries of Our Era.* New York, 1923–1958.

Tillyard, E. M. W. *The Elizabethan World Picture.* New York 1944.

Waters, David W. *The Art of Navigation in England in Elizabethan and Early Stuart Times.* London, 1958.

Wightman, W. P. D. *Science and the Renaissance.* Aberdeen, 1962.

TAISNIER, JEAN, B. 1509.

A very necessarie and profitable booke concerning nauigation, compiled in Latin by Ioannes Taisnierus . . . named a treatise of continuall motions. Translated into Englishe, by Richarde Eden.

Imprinted at London by Richard Iugge. [1579?]

Collation: 20 cm. (4to): ***^{8} A-D^8 E^2. [84] p.

Notes: Translation of Opusculum perpetua memoria dignissimum. Date of publication is based on Alden.

References: JCB Lib. Cat. Pre-1675, I:277; Alden, J. E. European Americana, 579/48; STC 23659.

JCB Library copy: Acq: 03395. Acquired before 1865. Call number: E579 T135v [F]. This copy is bound in contemporary vellum.

Tracings: 1. Navigation. I. Title. II. Title: A treatise of continuall motions.

¶ A very necessarie and
profitable Booke concer-
ning Nauigation, compiled in
Latin by Ioannes Taisnie-
rus, a publike professor
in Rome, Ferraria, & other
Uniuersities in Italie of
the Mathematicalles,
named a treatise of
continuall Mo-
tions.

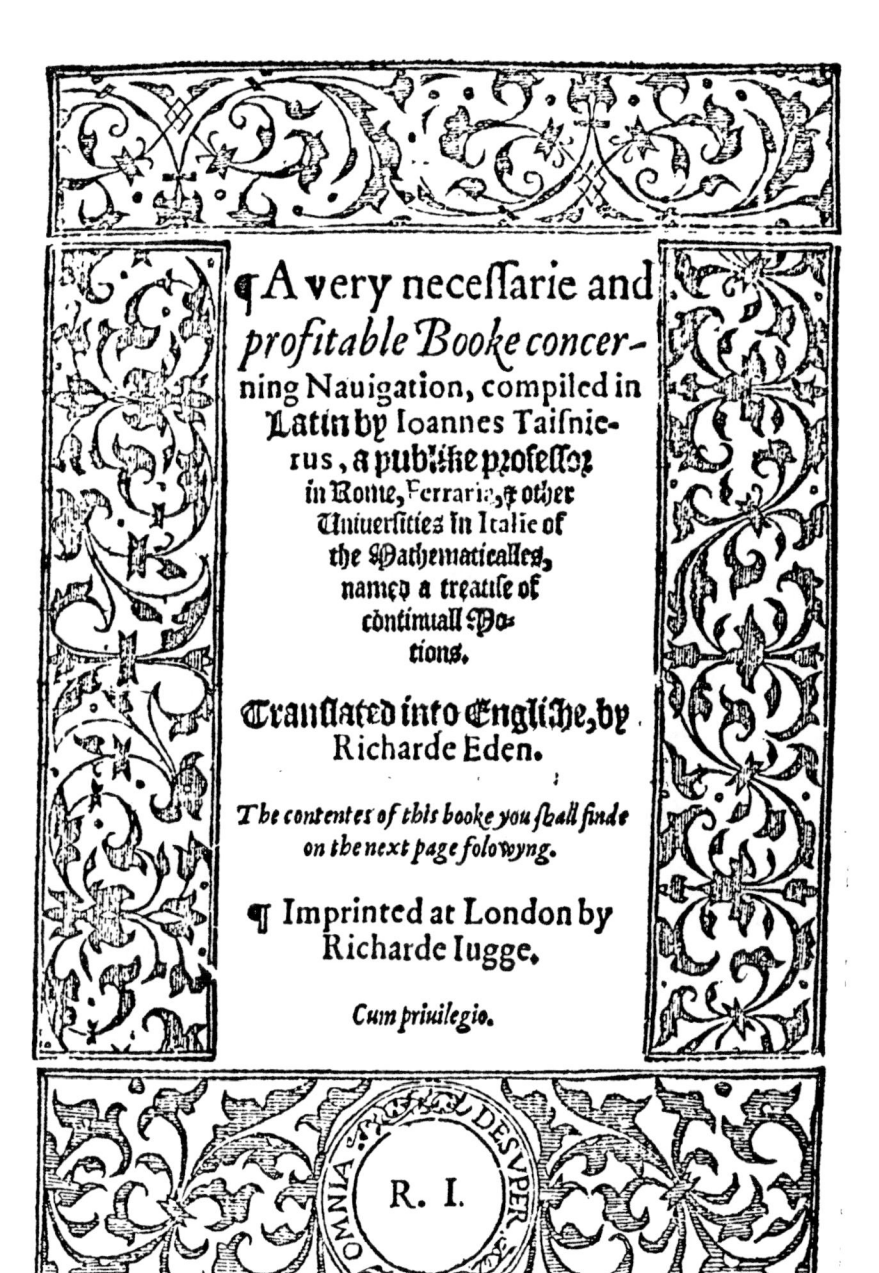

Translated into Englishe, by
Richarde Eden.

*The contentes of this booke you shall finde
on the next page folowyng.*

¶ Imprinted at London by
Richarde Iugge.

Cum priuilegio.

The Table.

1. Of the marueylous nature and vertue of the Lode stone, called in Latin Magnes, where they be found, and howe to knowe the best.

2. Of continual motion by the sayd stone, Magnes.

3. Of the due proportion of whatsoeuer Ship, and the disclosyng of certayne Mathematicall secretes.

4. Of ebbyng and flowyng, with their diuersities, and the causes thereof.

5. Demonstrations of proportion of motions local, confutyng the opinion of Aristotle therein.

The Epistle Dedicatorie.

To the ryght woorshipfull Syr *Wylliam Wynter, Knyght, Maister*
of the Ordinaunce of the Queenes Maiesties Shippes, and Surueyor of the sayd Shippes.
Richarde Eden wysheth health and prosperitie.

It is nowe about twelue yeeres paste (gentle Maister Wynter) since the curtesie and fauour which long before I founde at your hande, moouued me no lesse for the good wyll that I haue euer borne you and your vertues, to excogitate or deuise somethyng, within the compasse of my poore abilitie, that myght be a wittnesse, & as it were a seale, to testifie both that I haue not forgotten your gentlenesse, & also howe desyrous I am to pay the debtes of freendshyp which then I promised you, & also attempted to performe: But beyng at that tyme preuented, by meanes of my sodayne departyng out of Englande, with my good Lorde the Vidame, with whom I remayned for the space of ten yeeres, vntyll the calamities of that miserable countrey, with losse of goods, and danger of lyfe, hath dryuen me home agayne into my natiue countrey: Where fyndyng my selfe at some leysure, and desyrous to passe foorth parte of my tyme in some honest exercise, which myght be profytable to many, domagable to none, and a meanes to geat me newe freendes, the olde in my so long absence, in maner vtterly wasted: I chaunced in the meane tyme, to meete with my olde acquayntance and freend, Richard Iugge, Printer to the Queenes Maiestie, who had many yeeres before, printed the Booke of Marten Curtes, of the Art of Nauigation, by me translated out of the Spanysh tongue. Whereof, hauyng with him some conference, he declared that he woulde prynt that booke agayne, yf I woulde take the paynes to deuise some addition touchyng the same matter, that myght be ioyned thereto. At whiche tyme, hauyng with me in the Latine tongue, these bookes here folowyng prynted, whiche I brought with me out of Fraunce, I soone agreed to his honest request, to translate them into Englyshe: Whiche beyng accomplyshed, this onely remayned, accordyng to the common custome, to consecrate and dedicate the same to some worthie personage, whose fame, auchoritie, and dignitie, myght defende them from the euyll tongues of such as are more redie rather to reproout other mens dooynges, then to doo any good them selues. And therfore (gentle Maister Wynter) knowing your auctoritie and fame in well deseruyng, and honorable seruice vnto your Prince and Countrey, to be suche as all men thynke so well of, and so greatlye esteeme, to whom (rather then vnto you) may I dedicate this booke of Nauigation? In consyderation whereof, and the hope that I haue in your approoued curtesie, fauourably to accept this dedication, as proceeping from one that desyreth nothyng more then to doo you seruice, and remayne in your grace, I shall thynke my trauayle wel bestowed, and sufficiently recompenced, yf it shall please you to accept the same as thankfully, as I wyllyngly offer it vnto you. For yf there be any thyng in me, wherein I maye by good reason please my selfe, it is cheefely this,

.2 that

The Epistle Dedicatorie.

that I haue euer loued and honoured men of singuler vertue or qualitie, in what so euer laudable Art or Science, euen of those whereof I mee selfe haue litle knowledge, as are Geometrie, Astronomie, Architecture, Musicke, Payntyng, feates of Armes, inuentions of Ingens, and suche lyke: Of the whiche, this our age maye seeme not onely to contende with the Auncientes, but also in many goodly inuentions of Art and wyt, farre to excede them. For (not to speake agaynst all the maruey!ous inuentions of our tyme) what of theirs is to be compared to the Artes of Printyng, makyng of Gunnes, Fyre woorkes, of sundry kyndes of artificiall Fyres, of suche maruelous force, that mountaynes of moste harde rockes and stones, are not able to resyst their violence, but are by them broken in peeces, and throwen into the ayre with suche violence, that neyther the spirite of Demogorgon, or the thunderboltes of infernal Pluto can doo the lyke. What shoulde I here speake of the woonderfull inuentions of Fartalio, in his booke De Arte maiori? or of many other, whereof Vannucius Beringocius wryteth in his booke, entituled, Pyrotechnia. As touchyng whiche terrible inuentions, and the lyke, although some men be of opinion that they were inuented by the instigation of the deuyll, for the destruction of mankynde: yet other weyghyng the matter more indifferently, thynke that the inuention of Gunnes hath been the sauyng of many mens lyues, because before the vse of them, men were not woont so long tyme to lye batteryng in the bisiegyng of Townes or Fortresses, but in short space to come to hande strokes, and to foughten feeldes, to the great slaughter of great multitudes. And seeyng that nowe our enimies the Turkes, and other Infidels, haue the vse of these deuylyshe inuentions (as they name them) it may be thought requisite for vs, agaynst suche deuylles to vse also the lyke deuylyshe inuentions, lest refusyng the same, and geuyng place to euyl, we shoulde wyllyngly suffer the kyngdome of the deuyll to triumphe ouer vs, not otherwyse able to resyst, and much lesse to ouercome so puissant and horrible enimies (except besyde al hope) myght aryse in our defence some newe Moyses, or Elias, or the Priestes of Iericho, whiche onely with the noyse and sounde of Hornes or Trumpettes ouerthrewe the walles of the towne. Neyther wyl the example of Dauid and Goliath, or of Samson and the Philistines, serue our turne at this tyme, although I beleeue that the arme of the Lorde is not weakened, yf there lacked not a Moyses with his rodde, and woorthie Assystentes, which myght helpe to holde vp his weerye arme. But to returne to speake of ingens, and ingenious inuentions, whiche inuented and vsed to the glorie of God, and defence of his people, against the furie and tyrannie of Infidelles, they may as woorthyly be called the gyftes of God, as were the inuentions and Art of them that buylded eyther the Temple of Hierusalem, or the Arke of God: And yet is it there wrytten of those Artificers, that God gaue them the spirite of knowledge and cunnyng in suche Artes. And therefore I thynke it may also be sayde without offence, that the knowledge of Archimedes, and other men in suche commendable inuentions, are the gyftes of God, for as muche as the gyftes of God are free, and not bounde to any nation or person. And yf it may be graunted that the spirites of men, or the spirite of God in men, may be diuided (as was the spirite of Moyses to twelue other) or otherwyse that the spirites of dead men may reuiue in other (after the opinion and transanimation of Pythagoras) we may thynke that the soule of Archimedes was reuiued in Beson, that excellent Geometer of our tyme, whom I knewe in Fraunce the Maister of the engins to the Frenche kyng, Charles the nienth, vnder whom that lamentable slaughter at Paris was committed, in the whiche were slayne so many noble men. Whiche cruiltie the sayde Beson abhorryng, fled hyther into England, and

Exod. xxxv.
Bezaleel and
Ahaliab.

here

The Epistle Dedicatorie.

here dyed, in the yeere 1573. and left in witnesse of his excellencie in that Art, a booke in prynt, conteynyng the fourmes and portractes of sixtie engins of marueylous strange and profytable deuice, for diuers commodions and necessary vses. Of the whiche, for as muche as three of them, that is to meane, the. 54. 57. and 60. be engines chiefely parteynyng vnto Shyppes, it shall not be from my purpose here to make a briefe rehearsal of them. The. 54. therefore (as he wryteth) is an engin not vnlyke vnto that whiche in auncient tyme Archimedes inuented for the Syracusians, wherewith a man with the strength of onely one hande, by helpe of the instrument called Trispaston (which in our tongue some tal an endlesse Scrue, brought a Shyp of marueylous greatnesse from the lande into the sea, in the syght of kyng Hieron, and an infinite multitude, whiche with all their force coulde not doo the same. &c. Of the which also, our countrey man, Roger Bacon, a great Philosopher (and no Nicromancer, as that ignorant age slaundered him) seemed to haue had some knowledge: For in his booke of the marueylous power of Art and Nature, he maketh mention of an Instrument (as farre as I remember) no bygger then a mans hande, wherewith one man myght drawe to hym the strength of three hundred men. And I well remember, that at my beyng in Fraunce, I hearde credible reporte, that the Earle of Rocumdolfe, an Almaine, made an engin, wherewith the sayde kyng Charles when he was but. xvi. yeeres of age, lyfted from the grounde a weyght, whiche the strongest man in the courte was not able to remooue. Almoste the lyke deuice we see in the bendyng of a Crossebowe. Also at my being in Germanie in the citie of Strosburge, a woorthy and learned Gentleman, Monsieur de Saleno, tolde me that in that citie one had inuented an engin of iron, no bygger then a mans hande, whereunto fastenyng a rope, with a hooke of iron, and castyng the hooke vpon a wal, tree, or other place, where it myght take holde, he coulde with that engin lyft hym selfe vp to the wal, or other place. But to returne to the other two engines of Beson, parteynyng to our purpose. Therefore the. 60. fygure (as he there wryteth) is the inuention of an engin, scarsely credible, wherewith by ballance and easie motion, beyond the order of nature, a Shyp may be so framed and gouerned, that in the calme sea it shall moone forewarde, and in little wynde hasten the course, & in toomuch wynde temper and moderate the same: A thyng woorth the knowledge to a kyng, as he sayth. Of the thyrd engin, which is the. 57. fygure of his booke, he wryteth thus, An Artifice not yet diuulgate or set foorth, whiche placed in the pompe of a Shyp, whyther the water hath recourse, and mooued by the motion of the Shyp, with wheeles and weyghtes, dooth exactly shewe what space the Shyp hath gone. &c. By whiche description, some doo vnderstand that the knowledge of the longitude myght so be founde, a thyng doubtlesse greatly to be desyred, and hytherto not certaynely knowen, although Sebastian Cabot on his death bed tolde me that he had the knowledge thereof by diuine reuelation, yet so, that he myght not teache any man. But I thinke that the good olde man, in that extreme age, somewhat doted, and had not yet euen in the article of death, vtterly shaken of all worldlye vayne glorie. As touchyng whiche knowledge of the longitude, to speake a litle more by occasion nowe geuen, it shal not be from the purpose, to rehearse the saying of that excellent learned man, Iohannes Fernelius, in his incomparable booke De abditis rerum causis, where in the Preface to king Henrie of Fraunce, he wryteth in this maner. We haue put our helpyng hande to the Art of Nauigation and Geographie: forby obseruation of the houres of the Equinoctialles, we haue inuented howe, in what so euer region or place of the worlde a man shalbe, he may knowe in what longitude it is: which certaynly we haue not taken of the fountaynes of the ancientes, but fyrste, of all other (as I thynke) haue drawen it of our ryuers, as our

owne

Of this instrument, reade the Cosmolabe of Beson.

The Epistle Dedicatorie.

stonne inuention. &c. So that (saith he) whiche way so euer you turne your eyes, you may see that the posteritie hath not ryotously wasted the inheritance of Artes and sciences, left them by their predecessors, but haue greatly encreased the same, and inuented other: For certaynely, the multitude of thinges incomprehensible, is infinite, and so therfore inuentions must needes also be infinite, & without ende. And therefore, as touchyng this thing (sayth he) to speake freely what I thynke, they seeme to me to offende as muche, whiche contende that the auncientes haue inuented and comprehended al thynges, as doo they whiche attribute not vnto them the fyrst inuentions, so depryuyng them of theyr ryght possission. For wheras nowe by the benefite of almyghtie God (who hath geuen vs his Christe, and with hym all good thynges) the lyght of trueth shyneth in our vnderstandyng by godly inspiration, there is no iust cause why we shoulde in suche thynges thinke vs inferior to the auncientes. Of which Argument, who lysteth may reade more in the sayde Epistle of Fernelius. And for as much as I haue made mention of such *An instrument in motion a-* inuentions, it shal not be from the purpose, to describe the goodly instrumēt wher-*greeyng with* of Angelus Policianus in the fourth booke of Epistles to Franciscus Casa, wryteth in *the motion of* this maner, I haue receyued your Epistle, wherein you signifie vnto me, that you *heauen.* haue hearde of the strange engine or instrument Automaton inuented, and made of *Anno Dom.* late by one Laurence a Florentine: in the which is expressed the course and motti-*1584.* ons of the Planettes, comformable and agreeyng with the motions of heauen: And that (for as muche as the reporte therof is hardly beleeued) you greatly desyre that I should wryte vnto you, what certayne knowledge I haue of that thing, wherein I am redie to obey your request. And although nowe it be long since I sawe it, yet as farre as I beare in memorie, I wyll breefely declare the fourme, reason, and vse thereof. And yf the description of it shal seeme vnto you somewhat obscure, you shall not ascribe it altogeather to my declaration, but partly to the subtiltie & nouiltie of the thyng. It is in fourme of a square pyller, sharpe towarde the top, in maner of a Pyramis, of the height of almost three cubites: ouer or aboue it, in maner of a couer, is a flat or playne rounde plate of gylted copper, garnyshed with sundry colours, on whose other part is expressed the whole course of the Planets, and whose dimention or measure is somewhat shorter then a cubite, and is within turned or mooued with certayne litle denticle wheeles, an immouable circle comprehendyng the hyghest border or margent, and diuided with the spaces of xxiiii. houres within it, in the hyghest turnyng rundel, the twelue signes are discerned by three degrees. Further, within are seene eyght rundels, in maner all of one greatnesse. Of these, two obteyne the myddle poynt, the one fastened in the other, so that the lowest beyng somewhat bygger, representeth the Sunne, and the hygher the Moone. From the Sunne a beame commyng to the circle, sheweth in it the houres: and in the Zodiacke, the monethes, dayes, and number of degrees, and also the true and halfe motion of the Sunne. From the Moone also proceedth a pynne, or wyre, whiche beneathe or downwarde in the border or margent of the greatest rundell, sheweth the houres: and passyng by the center of the Epicicle of the Moone, and extendyng to the Zodiacke, sheweth the halfe motion of his Planet. Another also ryfyng from thence, and cuttyng the border of the center of the Moone (that is of the Epicicle) sheweth her true place, whereby are seene the slownesse, swyftnesse, al motions and courses, coniunctions also, and ful Moones. About these are syxe other rundels: of the whiche, one, whom they call the head and tayle of the Dragon, sheweth the Eclipses both of the Sunne and Moone. The other are attributed to the Planets: from euery of whiche, proceede two poyntes, assigning the motions (as we haue sayd) of the Moone: but they also goe backwarde, whiche channceth not in the Moone, whose Eclipse is mooued contrarywyse,

The Epistle Dedicatorie.

trarywyse. And thus the reason of coniunctions, departynges, and latitudes, is manifest in all. There is also an other border lyke vnto a Zodiacke, cutting or diuidyng vpwarde or aboue, those syxe litle rundels (whereof we haue spoken) being the rundels of the Planettes: whereby appeareth the degrees of the East signes, and the spaces of the daies (that is to say) at what houre the Sunne riseth, by the whiche, euery of the Planettes are carried in their rundels or circles by course, in the day tyme to the East, and in the nyght to the West. Agayne contrarywyse, the greatest rundel of al, draweth with it al the Planettes, in the nyght to the East and in the day to the West, in the space of. 24. houres. Al which, to agree with the motions of heauen, both reason and experience doo confyrme: And therfore ought ye not to marueyle, yf these thynges seeme incredible to many. For (as sayth the wyse Prouerbe) fayth is slowlye geuen to great thynges, for euen we scarsely beleeue our owne eyes, when we see suche thynges. And therefore, whereas in tyme past I read, that suche a lyke instrument was made by Archimedes, my sayth yet sayled me to geue credite to so great an Aucthour, which thyng neuertheless this our Florentine hath perfourmed. The worke doubtlesse beyng of such excellence, that all prayse is inferior to it, and can not therfore for the woorthynesse thereof be otherwyse praysed, then to say that it passeth all prayse. The Artificer him selfe also being a man of such integritie of maners, that the sunne is nothing inferior to the excellencie of his wyt: in so much that he may seeme a man sent from heauen, where he learned the makyng of this heauen, by the example of the other. Herberto Policianus. Of the lyke instrument, Roger Bacon also maketh mention in his sayde booke, of the marueylous power of Art and nature, affyrmyng the same to be woorth a kyngdome to a wyse man. But for as muche as the subiect whiche I haue nowe in hande, is cheefely touchyng inuentions parteinyng to Shyppes, and the Art of Nauigation, I thynke good to speake somewhat of the inuention of a certayne Italian wryter, named Leonardo Fiorananti, who in his booke, entituled, Specchio di scientia vniuersale, doeth greatly glory in the inuention of Shyppes, whiche can not peryshe eyther on the sea, or the lande, affyrmyng that the lyke was neuer inuented since the creation of the worlde. But I feare me, lest vayne glorie of discoursyng in the Italian tongue, hath caused him more then needes, to commende his owne inuention, as for the moste parte is the maner of the Italian wryters. Therfore committing the iudgement hereof to men of greater experience and knowledge in these thynges, I wyl onely translate his woordes, whereby in the booke before named, he describeth the sayde Shyppe in this maner. Take beames of Fyrre, or Pyne tree, which of their owne nature can neuer goe downe, or syncke, or abyde vnder the water, and with these brames frame an engine (Machina, yf I may so call it) of the length of three score foote, and of the breadth of twentie foote, and of the heyght of syxe foote, laying the fyrste ranke in length, and the other trauerse, or ouerthwarte, and the thyrde agayne in length, fashionyng the fore parte lyke vnto other Shyppes, and in lyke maner, bryngyng the poupe or hynder parte to good fourme: then with suche irons as apparteyne, bynde it, and strengthen it in suche maner that it can not breake. And vpon this frame or fundation buylde your Shyppe, of suche fashion as you thynke best. &c. It were here too long to rehearse with what proude woordes and ostentation he magnificeth this inuention. But whether this frame or engine shoulde be bylden vpon the keele or bottome of the Shyp, or otherwyse, I commit it to them of better iudgement, as I haue sayde. But wheras it may for this tyme suffise to haue wrytten thus muche of these thynges, I wyll make an ende with onely a breefe rehearsal of the inuention and encrease of the Art of Nauigation.

After that the Art of Nauigation was founde, euery man began to chalenge vnto hym

Lib.3. Ca.18
The inuention of a Shyp which can not be drowned.

The Epistle Dedicatorie.

hym the dominion of the sea, & there to dwel and kepe warre euen as on the land. Minos (as wryteth Strabo) was the fyrst that ruled on the sea, whiche neuertheleſſe, other aſcribe to Neptunus, who fyrst founde the Art of Nauigation, and was therefore (as wryteth Diodorus) appoynted by Saturnus to be Admiral of the fyrste Nauie: and thereby the poſteritie afterwarde aſcribed to him the gouernaunce of the ſea, and named him the God thereof. After whom the Cretenſes euer were eſteemed moſt expert in the Art of Nauigation. But (as wryteth Plinie) boates were fyrſt inuented, and with them was the fyrſte ſaylyng in the Ilandes of the redde ſea, vnder kyng Erythra, as alſo witneſſeth Quintilian, ſaying, If none had proceeded further then the inuentions of our predeceſſors, we had had nothyng in the Poets aboue Andronicus, and nothyng in hiſtories aboue the Annales or Cronicles of Byſhoppes, and had yet haue ſayled in troughes or in boates. Other haue aſcribed this inuention to diuers other nations and perſons, as to the Troians and Myſians in Helleſponto, and alſo that the ancient Britanes made boates of leather or hydes, and ſayled with them in the Ocean ſea. Plinie wryteth, that Danaus was the fyrſt that brought a Shyppe out of Grece into Egypt. Some alſo geue the ſame to Minerua. But moſt ryghtfully, the inuention both of the Shyp, and Art of Nauigation, is aſcribed to Noe, who (as wryteth Eusebius) was long before Neptune or Danaus. For doubteleſſe (ſayth he) the Arke of Noe was none other then a Shyp, and the fyrſte and onely exemplar of the buyldyng of all other Shyppes or veſſelles of ſaylyng. Alſo the moſte ancient wryter Beroſus the Chaldean (as wryteth Ioſephus) calleth the Arke of Noe, a Shyp. The ſame Ioſephus alſo ſayth, that the Nephues of Noe, departyng to inhabite diuers partes of the worlde, vſed many Shyppes. &c. Long after Noe, the Syrians were counted moſt expert in the Art of Nauigation: and after them, diuers other nations. For wheras no Art is ſo perfect, but may receyue encreaſe, hereof doth it folowe, that this Art alſo hath been greatly augmented, and brought to further perfection by witty inuentions of the poſteritie, euen vnto our age: wherof, who ſo lyſteth to knowe further more particulerly who inuented all other partes and inſtrumentes parteynyng to al ſortes of Shyppes, & Art of Nauigation, may reade ye thyrde booke of Polidor Virgil,
Cap xv, De Inuentorib.
Rer. and Bayſius,
de re nauali.

Thus gentle Maiſter Wynter, beſeechyng your woorſhyp to take in good part this teſtimonie of my thankfull hart (ſuche as it is) I beſeeche the immortall God to proſper all your dooinges to his honor, and the benefite of your Countrey

(*.*)

¶To the right Reuerende father in
Chriſte, and honorable Prince, Lorde
Iohn Gebhard, of the Earles of Mansfelt, &c,
Archbiſhop of Colen, Prince electer, duke
of Angaria and VVeſtphalia, hygh
Chaunceler of the Romayne
Empire, &c.

THE thing which to this day in maner from the beginning of the world, great Philoſophers with perpetual ſtudie and great labour, haue endeuoured to bring to effect, and deſired ende (moſt gratious Prince) bath neuertheleſſe hitherto remayned eyther vnknowen, or hydde, not without great damage and hynderance of moſte expert Mathematicians and Architectours, and al other men of lyke practicall faculties: And yf any there haue been whiche haue attayned to the experience of this continuall motion, I ſuppoſe the ſame to haue been vexed and noted, with the vayne glorye of the incomparable paynter and grauer, Michael Angelo, who euen at the extreme rendryng of the ſpirit of lyfe, dyd not vouchſafe to diſcloſe vnto his owne ſonne the ſecrets of his arte, eſteeming it greatly to the reputation of his fame and glory, by this ingrate hydyng of his ſcience, falſely to obteyne a perpetual memorie with ſuche as ſhoulde ſucceede hym: Or els truely be doubted (as is commonly ſeene in all maner of doctrine and ſcience) that there ſhoulde ſtill ryſe vp certayne malitious and enuious quarrelers, and troublous wits, inſtigate by an euyl ſpirite, to deface and ſuppreſſe trueth with ſlaunderous tongues, eſpecially agaynſt artes Mathematikes (of whiche kinde, are Grauyng, Payntyng, and ſuche lyke) whiche in al ages haue euer been ſubiect to this inconuenience of ignorant detractours, except they be defended by the protection and title of fauourable princes. And wheras ſuche ſciences

A perpetual or continuall motion.

Michael Angelo.

vnto

The Preface.

vnto the ignorant seeme ridiculus and suspicious, neuertheleſſe in the frame and experience of this continuall motion, ought no suspicion to be had. And forasmuche as the same is very neceſſarie and profitable for the common wealth, I was the bolder through confidence in your hyghnes clemencie vnder the grace and title of the same, to put foorth this litle booke of continuall motion. The whiche howe great profite and exercise it may bryng to excellent men of what so euer facultie, experience it selfe shal easily declare. Moſt humbly desiring your highneſſe, gratiously to accept this my trauaile with such as are conſecrate to the Muses, and employ theyr labours to the profite of mankinde.
(∴)

Your hyghneſſe moſte humble seruant and Oratour, Iohn Taiſnier Hamonius.

Of the nature and effectes of the Lode stone, called in Latine Magnes.

It is a common prouerbe that in stones, woodes, and hearbes, consisteth great vertue: which saying is doubtlesse most manifest by the dayly experience of this stone, beyng founde in sundry places of India, it is sayde also that it was founde in Spayne by one named Heracleon (as witnesseth Nicander) whyle in keepyng of cattell, the iron nayles of his showes and pyke of his staffe, cleft fast to the stone. Of the which Magnes, are fiue kindes as Sotacus wrpteth. That is to wyt: one of Ethiopia. An other of Macedonia. The thyrde is founde in Echio of Beotia. The fourth about Troades of Alexandria. The fyfth of Magnesia Asiæ. The difference of the stone is, whether it be male or female. The next difference, is in colour: for that which is founde in Macedonia and Magnesia, is ruddishe and blacke. That of Beotia, is more ruddish then blacke. That of Troades is blacke, and of female kinde, and therefore without vertue. The worst of Magnesia Asiæ, is whyte, and draweth not iron, and is lyke vnto a pumice stone. They are proued the best which are most of blewe or heauenly colour. That of Ethiope is most praysed, and (as Plinie sayth) is solde for the weight of siluer. This is founde in Zimri, a sandie region of Ethiope, where is also founde Hæmatites Magnes, of bloody colour, appearyng lyke blood yf it be grounde, and also lyke saffron, whiche in drawyng of iron, is not of like vertue to the Hematites Magnes of Ethiopia, whiche draweth vnto it an other Magnes. All these be profitable for medicines of the eyes, eche of them accordyng to their portion, and do specially stay Epiphoras (that is) droppyng of the eyes. And also beyng brunt or made in powder, they heale burninges. And not farre from the same place of Ethiopia, is a mountayne

Fiue kindes of Lode stones.
Lodestone male and female.
The best Lode stone of blewe colour.
Lode stone solde for the weight of siluer.
One lode stone draweth another.
Lode stones medicinable for the eyes.

whiche

The vertue of the Lode stone.

The Stone Theamedes putteth iron from it.

whiche bryngeth forth the stone called Theamedes, which putteth from it, and refuseth iron. I haue often prooued the vertue and power of the stone Magnes, by the needle whiche is in some Dialles, by the attraction thereof, moouyng it selfe from syde to syde, and rounde about. Although the stone were vnder a table, yet doeth the needle, being aboue the table, naturally folow the moouyng of the stone. It is therfore no marueyle yf there be great vertue in stones, woodes, and herbes. It hath also been prooued, that Shyppes compact with iron nayles, saylyng by the sea of Ethiope, and by tempest dryuen to lande, to certayne capes or landes endes, haue by these stones been eyther drawen to the bottome of the sea, or els the nayles beyng drawen out by the vertue of the stone, the Shyp hath fallen in a thousande peeces. And therefore the discreete and ware Cantabrians, most expert Mariners, saylyng by the sea of Ethiope, frame their Shyppes with pynnes and hoopes of wood, to auoyde the danger that myght chaunce of lyke occasion.

Iron nayles drawen out of Shippes by the stone.

Agayne, of the naure, knowledge, vertue, equalitie, qualitie, and effectes of the stone Magnes, or the Lode stone.

FOR as muche as euery thyng that is good, is so muche the better as it is more common: therefore doo I intende to communicate vnto our posteritie, this litle woorke of the nature, effects and miracles of the stone Magnes. The whiche, although they may seeme to the ignoraunt common people, to exceede the limittes of nature, yet to expert men, and Mathematitians, they seeme not so strange, notwithstandyng that it is almost impossible to manyfest al the secrets and miracles therof: For whereas Art inuenteth, and bryngeth to perfection many thynges whiche are impossible to nature, it is necessary that he who desyreth to doo great effectes in these thinges, and the lyke, be very expert in woorkyng with the hande: neyther is it sufficient for him to be a perfect Naturalist, Mathematitian, or Astronomer, for as muche as furthermore is requyred great dexteritie of handie woorke: And for defaulte hereof, it commeth to passe, that in this our age these natural artes lie hid & vnknowen.

Art in manye thyngs passeth and amendeth nature.

This

The vertue of the Lode stone.

This stone is knowen by colour, vertue, weyght, and equalitie. The best colour, is lyke pure iron, shynyng, mixt with Indian or heauenly colour, & is in maner like iron poolished. This stone is also oftentymes found in certayne regions of the North, & is brought from thence into certayne partes of Normandie and Flaunders. The experience of the vertue of this stone, is easie. For if it drawe vnto it a great weyght of iron, it is iudged to be stronge: & the heauier also the better. By equalitie, it is iudged yf it be al alyke of one substance and colour: but yf it be vnequall with chappes, & holow places indented, hauyng red spottes here and there, it is vnapt to the art of nauigation, or of continual motion. It representeth the similitude of heauen. For lyke as in heaue are two poynts immoueable, ending the axiltre of the sphere, vpon the which the whole frame of heauen is turned (as may be founde by the arte wherby Cristall & other stones are poolished:) euen so the stone Magnes, reduced into a globous or rounde forme, laying thereon a needle or any other lyke iron then which way so euer the needle turneth and resteth, thereby is shewed the place of the poles. And that this may be done more certaynely, it must be oftentymes attempted, and the lyne shewed by the needle, must be obserued: for such lynes shal cut the one the other in two pointes, as the Meridian circles ioyne togeather in the poles of the worlde.

The stone Magnes is knowen by colour, vertue, weyght, and equalitie.
Colour.
Vertue.
Equalitie.

Howe to finde the poles by the stone.

The same is geathered an other way.

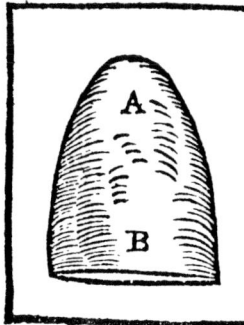

This is done more certaynely, yf in the round stone (as is sayd) be found the place which oftentimes draweth iron, whiche beyng founde, yf then the poynt do exactly appeare, part of the broken needle, muste be layde vpon the stone, and be so often by litle and litle transposed, vntyll the styple or pyn by perpendicle or plommet do directly fal vpon ye stone. For there on the contrary parte, by lyke maner shalbe found the other pole. A. shalbe the true point, and B. the false.

The vertue of the Lode stone.
The maner to knowe the one pole from the other.

Whiche of the two poyntes aforesayde may aunswcare to the pole Artike or the North pole, is founde in this maner Cause a large vessell to be fylled with water, in the which cause the stone Magnes to be layde vppon a lyght boorde, not deepe, muche lyke the coueryng of a boxe, so neuerthelesse that the two poyntes founde in the stone may lye equally eleuate in

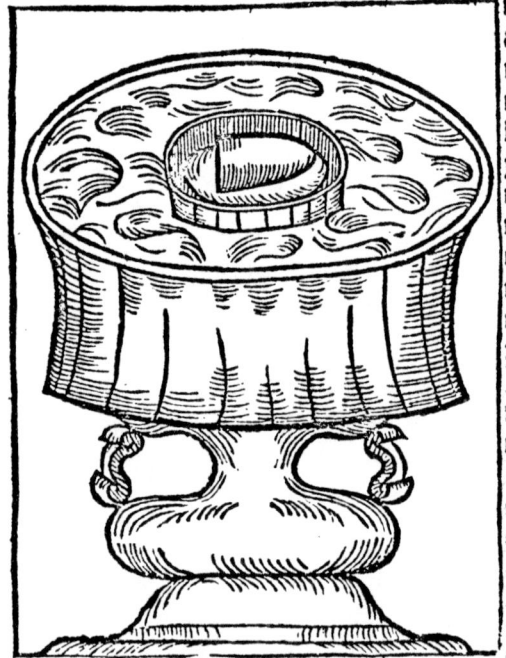

the sayd boxe: and so by vertue of ý stone, the boxe shalbe mooued to ý place where the meridionall pole shall extēde toward the South, & the other opposite to the North, & shal rest ther. And thus shal it be easye to discerne, whiche of the poynts answereth to the pole Artike, & to the pole Antartike, so that the places of heauen be fyrste knowen by anye meanes.

That

The vertue of the Lode stone.
That one stone draweth another.

How one stone draweth another, we wil declare hereafter. Lay ye one (as is sayd) vpon a boorde or bote in the water, that it may freely flote, & holde an other in your hande. If then the North part of the stone, whiche you holde in your hande, you turne to the South parte of that whiche floteth in the bote, or otherwise the South part to the North, the floting stone shall turne toward your hande: and yf contrarywyse, you turne the lyke part to his lyke, that is to say, the South part to the South &c. the floting stone shal flye from you. By this experience is destroyed the reason of certayne Phisitions, which dispute on this maner. If Scammonea drawe vnto it choler by similitude or lykenesse of nature, ergo muche more shoulde one Magnes draw another, rather then iron: for that which they assume falsely, we haue nowe taught to be true. The lyke iudgement is of a longe slender iron that is rubbed with this stone: for yf in the water it be layde on a lyght peece of wood, or a strawe, or such lyke, so that it may freely flote vpon the water, the one ende of it shall turne to the North, and the other to the South. And yf holdyng the stone in your hand, you turne his North poynt to the South extremitie or end, or contrarywise, the stone shal then draw iron. But contrarily, if you turne the lyke part to the lyke (as is aforesayd) it shall flye from the iron, or dryue it away. The reason whereof seemeth to be, that the agent doth not onely endeuour to make the patient lyke vnto it selfe, but also in such sort to vnite it with him selfe, y of them two be made one, as may appeare by this reason. Take the stone Magnes A D. of the which A signifieth the North poynt, and D. the South. Diuide the stone in two parts A B. and C D. put A B. to the water as is sayde, and by this meanes you shall see A. turne to the North, and B. to the South. For the breakyng

A question of attraction of humours &c.

Scammonea, and choler.

A yire or a needle.

A. The North part.
D. The South part.

How the stone draweth iron or driueth it away.

Agent and patient.

The stone diuided in the myddest.

The vertue of the Lode stone.

breakyng or diuidyng of the stone, diminish not the vertue therof, so that it be Homogenie, þ is, in all partes alike. Take therfore A B, for the patient, and C D, for the agent. Then wheras the agent, in the best maner it may, worketh to conserue the order of nature, it is manifest that D. can not draw C. the South: For although they coulde by that meanes be ioyned, yet shoulde there not so be made one of them two, the partes remaynyng in theyr vertue: for yf A. shoulde remayne North, then D. shoulde be South, whiche is certayne to haue the powre of the North.

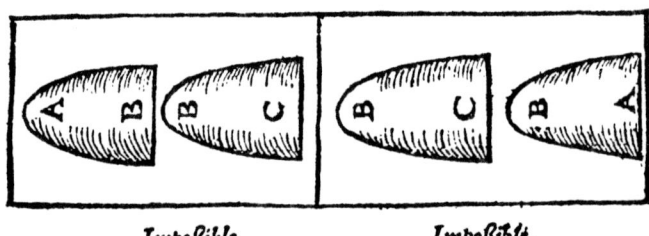

Impoßible.   *Impoßible.*

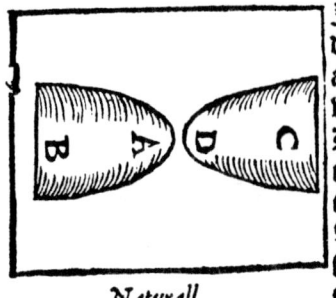

Naturall.

Neyther contrarīwyse shal C. draw A. for both are Northly, and so shoulde B be the North whiche fyrste was South, and D. in lyke maner: for so shoulde the order of nature be inuerted. It remaineth therfore that A. shal naturally draw D. & B. shal draw C. For so euery way shall remayne equall strength

From whence the stone hath his vertue. of al. Some ignorant men were of opinion that the vertue of the stone Magnes, commeth not of heauen, but rather of the nature of the place where it is engendred, sayinge that the mines thereof are founde in the North, and that therefore euer one part of the stone extendeth towarde North. But these are ignoraunt that this stone is also founde in other places. Wherof it shoulde folow that it shoulde then extende it selfe aswell to other and diuers partes, as to the North. Which thing is false, as is wel knowen

by

The vertue of the Lode stone.

by common experience, for it euer moueth to the North in what so euer place it be. Neyther is it to be beleeued, that the North starre of the Mariners is the Pole: for as muche as that starre is without the Meridian lyne, and but twyse within one reuolution of the fyrmament. But whereas the maruelous vertue of

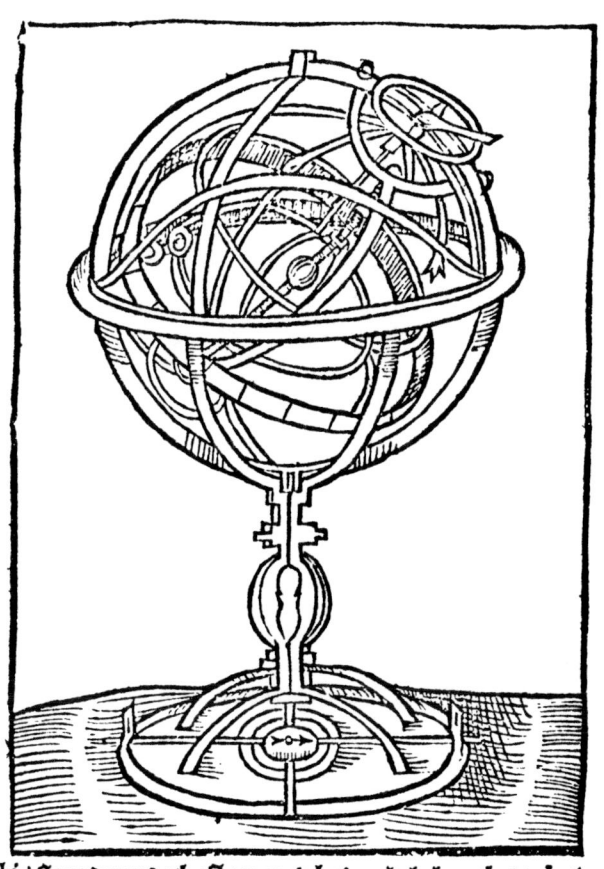

The North starre is not the Pole.

this stone dependeth of heauen, who would beleue that only two poyntes thereof shoulde so haue them selues, and not rather that euery parte of it should not enclyne to some lyke part in heauen, as may thus be prooued. Let the stone be brought into a Spherical

Euery part of this stone respecteth some part of heauen

A.i.

The vertue of the Lode stone.

rical or rounde fourme, as is sayde, and the Poles being founde in maner before declared, let it be turned vppon two pynnes, or Turners instruments, and there be pullyshed, vntyl it be on euery parte of equall heauynesse, which you may wel fynde by often prooupng: for that parte that falleth downe is heauiest, whiche done, frame it a Meridian circle with a Horizon, wherin fasten two other pynnes, vpon the whiche it may easyly mooue, and direct the Poles most exactly to the Poles of the world, the which yf it come wel to passe, reioyce that then you haue found almost one of the greatest miracles of natural thynges. For you shal by this meanes see the Ascendent, the place of the Sunne, and the lyke. &c. at euery moment. But yf it fal not out accordyng to your desyre, you ought not to impute that to the art, but to your owne ignoraunce and negligence. For yf you execute al thinges duely, accordyng to the art, you neede not to doubt the successe.

The greatest miracle in naturall thinges.

The composition of Instrumentes by the stone Magnes.

Howe by this stone instrumentes maye be framed, by the whiche may be founde the Azimuthes of the Sunne and Starres (that is to say, Vertical circles) it shal not be necessary to shewe, for as muche as the same is easily done by the Mariners Compasse, or by the boxe with the Magnes or Lode stone inclosed, and flotyng aboue the water with a pynne erected, and in the vppermoste parte diuided into 360 partes, after the maner of Astronomie.

Of

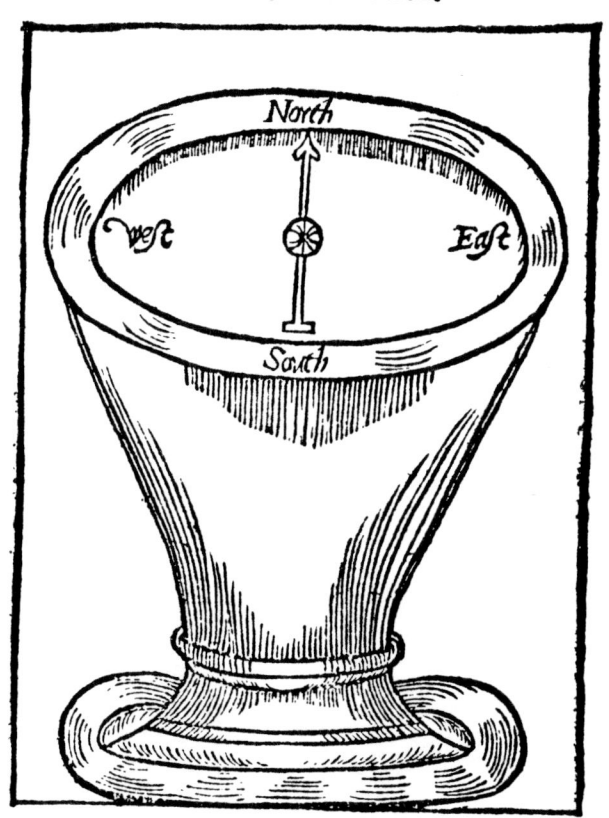

Of conntinuall motion.

Of continual motion.

From the begynnyng of the worlde, in maner all naturall Philosophers and Mathematitians, with great expences and labour, haue attempted to fynde out a continuall motion or moouyng: yet vnto this day haue fewe or none atteyned to the true ende of their desyre. They haue attempted to doo this with diuers instrumentes & wheeles, and with quickſyluer, not knowyng the vertue of this stone. Neyther can conti-

A ij　　　　　　　　　　　nual

The vertue of the Lode stone.

nual motion be founde by anye other meanes, then by the stone Magnes, in this maner. Make a holowe case of sylver, after the fashion of a concaue glasse, outwardly laboured with curious art of grauyng, not onely for ornament, but also for lyghtnesse, for the lyghter that it is, so much the more easyer shal it be mooued, neyther must it be so pearced through, that such as are ignorant of the hyd secrete, may easly perceyue it.

The fourme of the stone.

The Pole   The Pole

It must haue on the inner syde certayne litle naples & denticles or smal teeth of iron of one equal weyght, to be fastened on the border or margent, so that the one be no further distant from the other, then is the thycknesse of a beane or chicke pease. The sayd wheele also must be in all partes of equal weyght, then fasten the Exiltree in the myddest, vpon the whiche the wheele may turne, the Exiltree remaynyng vtterly immooueable. To the whiche Exiltree agayne shalbe ioyned a pynne of sylver, fastened to the same

The vertue of the Lode stone.

same, and placed betweene the two cases in the hyghest parte, whereon place the stone Magnes. Beyng thus prepared, let it be fyrste brought to a rounde fourme, then (as is sayd) let the Poles be founde: then the Poles vntouched, the two contrarye

sydes lying betwene the Poles, must be fyled and pullyshed, and the stone brought in maner to the fourme of an egge, and somewhat narower in those two sydes, lest the lower parte thereof shoulde occupie the inferior place, that it may touche the walles of the case lyke a litle wheele. This done, place the stone vpon the pynne, as a stone is fastened in a ryng, with suche art, that the North Pole may a litle enclyne toward the denticles, to the

Denticles be litle teethe, or pynnes about the wheele, that it maye the easier turne about.

A iii ende

The vertue of the Lode stone.

ende that the vertue thereof worke not directly his impression, but with a certayne inclination geue his influence vpon the denticles of iron. Euery denticle therfore shall come to the North Pole, and when by force of the wheele it shall somewhat passe that Pole, it shall come to the South part, whiche shall dryue it backe agayne: whom then agayne the Pole Artike shall drawe as appeareth. And that the wheele may the sooner doo his office within the cases, inclose therein a litle Calculus (that is) a litle

Calculus, a litle rounde stone or small weyght lyke a pellet or plommet.

A. *The stone.*

B. *The siluer pinne.*

E. *Calculus.*

rounde stone or pellet of copper or syluer, of suche quantitie, that it may commodiously be receyued within any of the denticles: then

The vertue of the Lode stone.

then when the wheeles shalbe raysed vp, the pellet or rounde weyght shall fal on the contrary parte. And whereas the motion of the wheele downewarde to the lowest part, is perpetuall, and the fall of the pellet, opposite or contrary, euer receyued within any two of the venticles, the motion shalbe perpetuall, because the weyght of the wheele and pellet euer enclyneth to the centre of the earth, and lowest place. Therfore when it shal permit the venticles to rest about the stone, then shall it well serue to the purpose. The myddle places within the venticles ought so artificially to be made holowe, that they may aptly receiue the fallyng pellet or plommet, as the fygure aboue declareth. And briefly to haue wrytten thus much of continual motion, may suffice.

(∴)

A iiij   Of

Of most swift Motion by arte of Nauigation.

WE intende nowe to speake of moste swyft motion, which to the cōmon sorte of men seemeeth incredible, for that the same maye be doone by saylyng in a shyp or other vessell, agaynst what so euer moste outragious course of any fludde or ryuer, and agaynst most furious wyndes what so euer they be, euen also in deepest wynter and greatest sourges of waters. Neyther is it maruayle yf this be incredible to the vnexpert. For the common people counteth that for a miracle, which the expert Mathematitians knowe to be naturall and easie: for yf it shoulde be propounded to the ignoraunt people, that anye man myght in the myddest of the waters and fluddes, descende to the bottome of the ryuer of Rene, his apparel remaynyng drye, & no part of his body wette, & also to bryng with hym burnyng fire from the bottome of the water, it shoulde seeme to them a laughyng stocke, a mockerie, and impossible. Whiche neuerthelesse in the yeere 1538. in Toleto a citie of Spayne, in the most swyft riuer Tagus (in the whiche golde is founde) runnyng agaynst the course of the Sunne none otherwyse then Danubius, and three other in the world, makyng theyr course from the west to the East, I, with twelue thousand other persons, saw in the presence of Charles the Emperour the fyfth of that name. Of such other maruaylous naturall experimentes, I neede not here to speake muche. Other there be that dare affirme, that a certaine ship was in such sort dryuen with violent wyndes and furious seas with so swyfte a course, that the Pilote standyng in the keele of the shyp, neare vnto the mast, shootyng an arrowe out of a crosse bowe, the arrowe fel downe before his feete, and came not so farre as to the forepart or forecastle of the shyp. I haue hearde also of credible men,

A strang experiment practised.

The ryuers of Tagus & Danubius.

Maruey!ous swiftnesse of a shyp.

Of certayne Mathematicall secretes.

men, that a certayne Pilote Cantabriar, lying at anker at Antwerpe, on a certayne Sunday after mornyng prayer, departed with full sayles and prosperous wyndes, vntyll he came to the coast of Saint James in Compostella. And immediatelp returnyng with lyke prosperous wyndes, came agayne to Antwerpe in the same shyp the Sunday next folowyng. The whiche I denye not, but may be done, yet not without great daunger of shipwracke, especially in the returne, the winde beyng at the South. Also in the yeere. 1551. I had experience of a most swyft motion. For, from Drepan of Sicilia and Trinacria, the porte of the galles of Maltha (nowe being in place of the Rhodes, otherwyse called of Saint John in Ierusalem) a certayne shyp without euer strykyng sayle, in. 37. houres arryued at Naples. And yet are these places distant in latitude almost fyue degrees, besyde some part of longitude: whiche on the earth corespondeth or amounteth to foure hundred and fyue myles. These motions, are caused by violent fluddes and outragious wyndes. The lyke also may be doone agaynst the furie of wyndes and violence of fluddes, when neede shalbe for expedite cariage of vitayles by sea, and euen in places where it is harde to come to lande, and this with small labour, as hereafter I wyll playnely declare by Demonstration: but oftentymes, most expert Pilotes and sea men, do marueyle that saylyng in shyppes of the selfe same makyng, weyght, content, or capacitie, framed also of the selfe same shyppwryght, furnished with equall sayles, and all other thynges apparteining, yet to be of such diuers swiftnesse, that the one can not kepe equal course with the other. Which maruelling doubtlesse proceedeth of ignorance and lacke of knowledge of the due proportion of the frame of al sortes of shippes: that is to meane, the deapth, breadth, heyght, and length (named by the maisters, latitude, longitude, altitude, and profunditie.) The which yf they be vnknowen to the maister Carpenter or Shyppwryght, two shyppes can neuer be so directed by equall course, but that one shalbe swyfter then another, as I playnely obserued in the expeditions of Arsenaria, or Thunes, or Agolette: in which amongst in maner innumerable shyppes, and especially Galleys, and foystes,

Swyfte speede after mornyng prayer.

An other experience of swift saylyng.

The differēce of shyppes in saylyng.

The proportiō in framyng of shyppes.

Tunes and Goletto.

Of the due proportion

ſopſtes, were ſcarſely two oꝛ one of the ſame quantitie, heauyneſſe, greatneſſe, and capacitie, oꝛ dꝛyuen all with one wynde and equall ſayles, that kept equall courſe one with another: And this doubtleſſe onely by reaſon of the different proportion of the frampyng, makyng, oꝛ architecture.

Of the ryght and due proportion of what ſo euer Shyppe.

IN the framyng of any maner of ſhyppe, the proportion of length, breadth, heyght, and deapth, ought moſt cheefely to be exactly obſerued, leſt the ignoꝛance and negligence of theſe conſyderations, ſhoulde hynder the ſwyfte courſe, and cauſe daunger of ſhypwꝛacke. The due proportion therefore of ſhyppes is, that fyrſte the longitude oꝛ length of the ſhyppe oꝛ veſſell what ſo euer it be, moꝛe oꝛ leſſe, ought to be diuided into 300 equall partes, as appeareth in the figure folowyng.

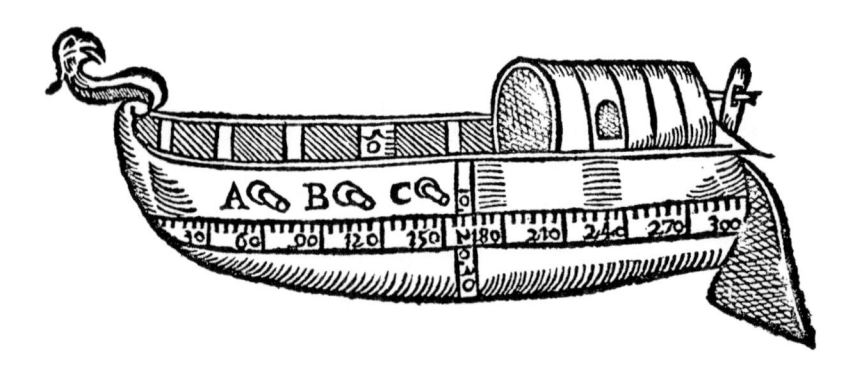

Of the whiche partes, 30. muſt be aſſigned to the heyght oꝛ deapth

of what so euer Shyppe.

depth, for the tenth part of y^e whole requisite longitude or length: and to the latitude or breadth shall corresponde the partes of the sayde longitude. 50. or the syxth part of the longitude. The matter also or tymber of the Shyp must be lyght, lest too muche heauynesse of the matter shoulde hynder the swyfte course. And this proportion of Shyppes or other saylyng vesselles, of whatsoeuer shape or frame, is most conuenient, and no lesse necessary: As for Scafes, Shyppes of burden, Galleis, double, triple, or quadruple (that is to say) of two, three, or foure men to an Ore. Also for Foystes, Pinaces, Brigantines, Espions, and suche lyke.

Of the framyng and Architecture of the aforesayde Shyp.

I HAUE often tymes attempted by Mathematical reason, howe and in what maner a commodious fashion of Shyppes, or other lyke vesselles may be inuented with smal labour and litle cost, which may in short tyme stryue against ye course of whatsoeuer strong fluddes or ryuers, as Rhene, Danubie, Mosella, Scalda, and almost infinite suche other, boylyng and ouerflowyng, through the abundance of great showres, molten snowes, and furious wyndes, and this especially for the commoditie of transportyng victualles, and suche other necessaries: In consyderation wherof, the proportion fyrst obserued, and the sayde Shyp or vessell almoste finished, then must be made three holes from the Kele, towarde the forecastle or foremoste part of the Shyp, as appeareth in the fygure by the letters A B C. In which holes, in tyme of the course, certayne engines of strange and marueylous inuentions may be fastened. In the poupe or hynder parte of the Shyp, maye be prepared (after the maner of Germanie) a litle Stoue or whotte house, where the Passengers maye commodiously rest. Nowe the Shyp beyng thus

Of certayne Mathematical secretes.

thus prepared, the bottome thereof must be dressed with tallowe, and not with tarre, that it may mooue the swyftlyer.

Thus hauyng absolued the frame and proportion of the sayde Shyp, the rest of Mechanicall or handicrafte woorke, we leaue to the Carpenters and Shyppwryghtes.

To what vse such kinde of Shyppes or vesselles may be applyed.

It chaunceth often tymes, and especially in winter, that certayne floods and riuers ouerflowen with to much abundance of waters, doo with their violence refuse all nauigations that may be made agaynst their course, to the great domage and hurt of the Inhabitantes of many Townes and Cities, to the whiche they shoulde carrie victuailes, and other prouisions, agaynst the course of the ryuers: And therefore in fauour of the common wealth, I haue inuented these kynde of Shyppes, that I may hereby, as by my seale, confyrme the good wyll I beare to our posteritie. Nowe therefore it may suffice to haue sayde thus muche of this swyfte motion whiche I haue proued with myne owne strength, and haue sufficiently declared the framyng and vse thereof: whereunto it shalbe easye for all men to adde more, accordyng to the excellencie of their wyttes and experience. For in all sciences it is easyer to adde to inuentions, then to inuent. Consyder nowe what commoditie this may bryng to the Brabantines, saylyng from Antwerpe to Bruxels in the newe ryuer: For that whiche they attempt dangerously with great vexation and shoggyng in waggons by foule and tedious iourney, often wette to the skyn for the space of one whole day, maye by water be doone more conueniently, in the space of foure or fyue houres, euen agaynst the ryuer and wynde.

It is easier to adde to inuentions, then to inuent.

The newe ryuer from Antwerpe to Bruxels.

And

Of certayne Mathematicall secretes.

And leste the reader shoulde seeme to refute our sayinges, whyle he thynketh those thynges whiche he esteemeth for miracles, to exceede the limittes of nature, I wyll shewe manifestly by one Demonstration, howe a man may descende into the bottome of anye water or ryuer, his body remaynyng drye, as here before I haue affirmed, that I sawe in the famous Towne and kyngdome of Toledo, before the Emperour Charles the fyfth, and infinite other. But here muste fyrste be consydered, that naturally the water or sea (as other Elementes) intendeth to Sphericall forme, and with his globosite or rysing, ouerpasseth moste hygh mountaynes. But agayne here shall ryse an other doubt to the vnexpert. That is: If the sea be hygher then the lande, howe is it then that it dooth not drowne and couer the earth? Whereunto I aunsweare, that the dryenesse of the earth maye so long respite the moystenesse of the water, vntyll it receiue or imbibe to muche moystenesse, whiche may thus be naturally prooued. Fyll a cuppe or other vessell with water or wyne to the brymme, so that the fulnesse thereof maye seeme to swell as though it woulde ouerflowe the brymme of the cuppe. Then may you yet put therein many peeces of golde, without sheddyng of one droppe of water. But yf the extremitie of the brymme be once wette, immediately the water ouerfloweth, because the dryenesse of the vessell dooth participate the moystenesse of the water: whiche is yet better prooued in maner as foloweth. Take a certayne quantitie of water, and spryncle it by droppes vppon a drye (or dustie) table: so shall the droppes partly shewe a Sphericall and swellyng forme remaynyng. But yf the table before be neuer so lyttle wette with water, the droppes spryncled thereon, shall flote abrode, and keepe no Sphericall or rounde forme, by reason of the moystnesse whiche the table had before receiued of the water. It hath also oftentymes chaunced, that certayne Townes and landes haue ben drowned by ouerflowyng of ryuers neare vnto them. Neuerthelesse, howe muche so euer suche waters increase and ryse, there is no daunger, vntyll great showres fallyng from heauen, doo thorowly wette the banckes, rampertes,

A notable experiment.

The water intendeth to globus forme.

Why the water dooth not ouerflowe the lande.

An experimēt.

The drowning of certayne Regions.

Of certayne Mathematicall secretes.

or valleys of suche riuers. For when they (as we haue sayde) be thorowly imbibed with moystenesse, they cause the ouerflowyng and breache, whereof foloweth the ouerflowyng and drownyng of the region: and this may suffise for aduertisement. Nowe therefore I come to the experience aforesayde, shewed at Toleto by two Greekes: who takyng a chaulderon of great capasitie, and the mouth turned downewarde, and so hangyng it in the ayre by ropes, they fasten certayne postes and boordes or shelues in the myddest of the chaldron where they place themselues with the fyre. Then to make it hang stedfastly and equally, they compasse the circumference, brymme, or border thereof with leaden plommetes on euery syde equally, and made of equal weyght, least any part of the circumference of the mouth of the chaldron when it is equally and softly let downe into the water, shoulde sooner touche the water then the whole circumference. For so shoulde the water easly ouercome the ayre inclosed in the chaldron, and resolue it into moysture. But yf by due proportion the chaldron thus prepared, be fayre and softely let downe into the water, the ayre inclosed in the chaldron (by resistance of the water) shall violently make hym selfe place, not admittyng the water to enter. So the men there inclosed, shall so long remayne drye in the myddest of the water, vntyll successe of tyme doo by respiration debilitate and consume the inclosed ayre, turnyng it into grosse humiditie ingrossed by the coldnesse and moystnesse of the water: but yf in due tyme the chaldron be softly and equally drawen out of the water, the men shal remaine drye, and the fyre not extinct, whiche also may thus be prooued: Take a cuppe of glasse of a certayne quantitie: the circumference of the mouth wherof, shalbe broder then the circumference of the bottome. In the mouth let be fastened a little sticke, tying thereto a threede: On the stycke, fasten a little candle of waxe, whose lyght may come onely to the myddest of the cuppe, least to muche nearenesse of the water myght suffocate the candle. Then proportionally (as in the former experiment) put the cup with the burnyng candle into a vessel ful of water, & in due tyme drawe it out softly and equally, so that no part of the mouth of the circumfe-

This experiment may be proued with a great bell.

Another example of the foresayd experiment.

Of certayne Mathematicall secretes.

circumference therof be drawen out before the whole, or spedely: so shall the candle remayne alyue, as it was before. These be naturall and Mathematicall Demonstrations. Let not therefore the ignoraunt condemne our wrytynges, before they knowe what maye be doone by experience. It is nowe then no more a miracle, when it is knowen to be naturall: And thus is it in all other Sciences and experimentes, whiche the common people thynke to be impossible. As the lyke in growyng of certayne fruites, trees, and herbes, by also helpyng nature, that they may spryng and growe before their naturall tyme, euen in the harte of Wynter. It seemeth also a miracle to the common people, that in the tyme of moste temperate season, and great calmenesse on the sea, Shyppes be helde faste immouable in the myddest of the sea, and sodaynely swalowed into the bowelles of the earth: whiche neuerthelesse is doone naturally in maner of an earthquake, and by lyke natural cause. The reason whereof, is, that the ayre as a moste lyght Element, inclosed in the bowelles of the earth, striuyng euer naturally to the circumference of the earth, as vnto his owne region. But the pores of the earth beyng strongly stopped, and the ayre thereby agaynst his nature forcibly inclosed, stryueth by violence to brust foorth, and so cleauyng the earth in the bottome of the sea, and great abundance of water fallyng into the breache, euen from the hyghest parte of the sea in that place, with swalowyng attraction of the fall, draweth downe with it sodainly the Ship or Shyppes, whiche at that tyme approcheth neare vnto the place of that whyrlepoole. Furthermore, anye ignoraunt man woulde hardly beleeue that the salt water of the sea maye be made freshe, and potable to be dronke, whiche neuerthelesse maye be doone naturallye, as hath been often prooued dyuers wayes. Some doo this (as is wrytten in Gemma Philosophica) puttyng the salte water in a vessell playstered or crusted ouer with cleane Waxe, whiche distyllyng through

A secrete knowen, is no more a miracle.

Ignorance causeth admiratiō

Whirlepooles deuouryng Shyppes.

The lyke of earthquakes, Gunnes, and vnderminyng.

The spirite of Demogorgon.

To make salt water freshe.

Of certayne Mathematicall secretes,
through the strayte and narowe pores therof, leaueth the
salt, which for his grosnesse can not passe therby. The
same may be done better by a Canon or Pype,
fylled with grauell or litle stones, and
that the salt water powred thereon, may diuers times passe
through that Pype
into an other
vessell.

*There is a bet-
ter way.*

¶ Of the Flowing, and Reflowing, (that is) increase and decrease of the Sea, with the causes therof, *more exactly then hytherto hath been declared by any.*

Heras heretofore mention hath ben made of the sea and flowyng of waters, and diuers other motions, it may be conuenient to adde hereunto the sayinges and wrytynges of the most expert and learned man, Fredericus Delphinus, Doctor of artes and phisicke, and publique professor of Mathematical sciences in the famous vniuersitie of Padua, touchyng the flowyng & reflowyng, or increase and decrease, (otherwise also named accesse and recesse, that is, commyng and goyng, or ebbyng and flowing) of the water of the sea. Which flowyng and reflowyng, some do also name, the false rest or quietnesse, or inordinate motion of the water of the sea. And albeit diuers learned men haue intreated of this matter, yet forasmuche as some of theyr wrytynges are somewhat darke, and not easie of all men to be vnderstoode, I haue thought it necessarye, partly out of theyr wrytinges, and partly by mine owne industrie, more clearly & largely to entreat hereof, that the same may be the better vnderstoode of all men.

Therfore, for the more easie vnderstandyng of these two maners of motions of the water of the sea, folowyng the mouyng of the Sunne and Moone, to the mouing of (primum mobile) the fyrst moueable, is fyrst to be knowen, that wheresoeuer a man is on the earth, his Horizon (as I haue said before in my treatise of the sphere) euer cutteth or diuideth to him the heauen into two halfes, & the one halfe of heauen is euer aboue his Horizon, and the other halfe beneath. And whereas in the halfe of a sphericall or rounde body, are conteyned two quarters, two quarters shall

Diuisio of heauen and the Horizon.

The Horizon diuideth heauen into two euer partes.

B j

A figure shewyng the beginning of the day increase at the Sunne risyng, and the beginning of the day decrease in the midday, and the beginning of the night increase at the Sunne setting, and the beginning of the night decrease at midnight.

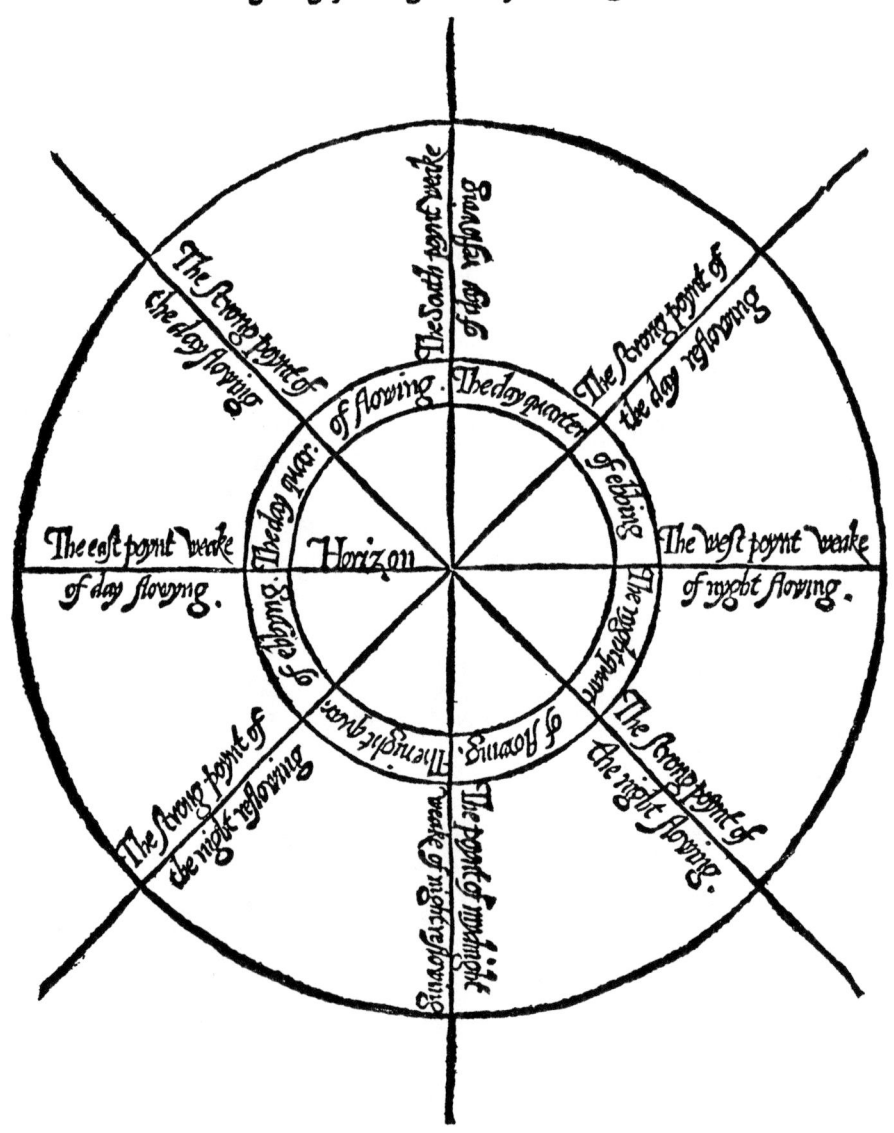

and reflowyng.

euer be aboue his Horizon, & two beneath. Those that are aboue the Horizon, are called diurnall or day quarters: & they that are vnder the Horizon, are called nocturnall or nyght quarters. Of these foure quarters of heauen, are two in the which is made the flowyng or increase of the water of the sea: and other two in the which is made the reflowing or decrease of the sea. The quarters in the which is made the flowing, is the quarter whiche is from the East to the South aboue the Horizon, whiche is the quarter of the day accesse, or increase of the day: and the quarter opposite or contrary, which is from the West to midnight vnder the Horizon, is the quarter of the nyght accesse. The quarters in which is made the reflowyng or decrease, is the quarter which is from the South to the West aboue the Horizon, which is the quarter of the recesse of the day: and the quarter opposite, which is from mydnyght to the East vnder the Horizon, is the quarter of the recesse of the nyght. &c.

Secondaryly, is also to be knowen, that there be in heauen eyght poyntes for the flowyng and reflowyng, or increase and decrease of the sea: of the whiche, foure are strong, and foure weake. Of the weake, two are weake for the flowyng, and two for the reflowyng. Weake for flowyng, are the poynt of the East, and poynt of the West, whiche are the begynnyng of the two quarters of flowyng. Weake for reflowyng, are the poynt of the South or mydday, and the poynt of mydnyght, whiche are the begynmynges of the two quarters of reflowyng: and these foure poyntes are distant the one from the other, by a quarter of heauen. Of the strong poyntes, two are strong for flowyng, and two for reflowyng. Strong for the flowyng, are the middle poynt betweene the East and the South in the daye quarter of flowyng, beyng distant from the East 45. degrees, and from the South lykewyse: And the middle poynt betwene the West and mydnyght, in the nyght quarter of flowyng, beyng distant from the West 45. degrees, and from mydnyght lykewyse. Poyntes strong for the reflowyng, is the myddle poynt, betweene South and West, in the day quarter of the reflowyng, beyng distant from the South 45. degrees, and from the West lykewyse: And the myddle poynt betweene midnight

Eyght poyntes of heauen for flowyng and reflowyng.

B ii and

Of flowyng,

A right Horizon is when both the poles lye in the Horizon, & that is to them only which dwell vnder the Equinoctiall. Poyntes of equall vertue in moouyng the water of the sea.

and the East, in the quarter of the nyght reflowyng, beyng distant from mydnyght. 45. degrees, and from the East lykewyse. And as the weake poyntes are distant one from the other by a quarter of heauen, so are also the strong poyntes distant the one from the other by a quarter of heauen, to them that haue a ryght Horizon.

It is thyrdly to be knowen, that beside the aforesayde eyght poyntes, to suche as haue a ryght Horizon, there be many other poyntes equipollent or of equall vertue. And suche be all the poyntes of heauen equally distant from the foure principal poyntes of heauen, whiche foure principall poyntes are, the poynt of the East, poynt of the West, poynt of the South, and poynt of mydnyght, or from the foure strong poyntes of heauen, whiche is all one, yet in quarters of contrarie operation. For all suche poyntes are equipollent or of equall vertue in moouyng the water of the sea: but in a ryght Horizon it is otherwyse, as shal appeare hereafter.

The aspectes whiche the Moone maketh with the Sunne euery moneth.

It is fourthly to be knowen, that the Sunne and Moone euery moneth, are togeather in one signe, degree, and minute. And this so beyng, is called the Coniunction of the Moone with the Sunne. From thence for the space of eyght dayes, or there about, the Moone is departed from the Sunne by her proper motion by a fourth part of heauen: and this departyng is called the fyrste quarter of the Moone with the Sunne. From thence in fourteene dayes, or thereabout, she is departed from the sunne by an other fourth parte of heauen, and so by the halfe of heauen: and this distance is called the opposition of the Moone with the Sunne, or the ful Moone. From thence to 21. dayes or thereabout, she is departed from her opposition with the sunne or full Moone by an other fourth part of the heauen, commyng towarde the Sunne: and this distance is called the seconde quadrature of the Moone with the Sunne, and then the Moone is distant from the Sunne by a fourth parte of heauen, as it was distant in the fyrste quarter, and so commeth neare to Coniunction with the Sunne. From thence at thyrtie dayes, or thereabout, the Moone is agayne with the Sunne in coniunction, as it was fyrst.

Fystly

and reflowyng.

Fyrstly and lastly, is to be knowen that the Sunne & Moone, both togeather euery naturall day (whiche is the tyme of. 24. houres, to the mouyng of the fyrst moueable) are the causes of flowyng and reflowyng, or increase and decrease of the water of the sea twyse. These declarations premised, and wel kept in memorie, let vs declare howe the Sunne and Moone both togeather euery naturall day, to the moouyng of the fyrste moueable, are the causes of the flowyng and reflowyng of the sea. For yf these declarations be well helde in memorie, and especially the quarters of heauen in whiche is the flowyng, and the quarters of heauen in whiche is the reflowyng, and whiche are the strong poyntes for the flowyng, and strong poyntes for the reflowyng, and whiche be the weake poyntes for the flowyng, and the weake poyntes for the reflowyng: these (I say) beyng kept in memorie, al the narration of the mouyng, and falle quietnesse of the sea, shalbe cleare and manifest. *The Sunne & Moone are the only causes of ebbyng and flowyng.*

Fyrst of all (as touchyng the flowyng and reflowyng of the sea to the mouing of the first moueable) it is to be knowen, that when the Sunne and Moone are ioyned togeather, which coniunction is called Nouilunium (that is) the new Moone, when they be moued to the moouyng of the fyrste moueable (called Primum mobile) from the East to the South, because the vertues both of the Sunne and Moone be vnite togeather, and both these Luminaries are moued continually to the moouyng of the first moueable by the quarter of the day flowyng, whiche is from the East to the West, the day flowyng or increase of the sea is continuall. And whyle they are moued frō the South to the West, because they are moued continuall by the day quarter of the reflowyng, the reflowyng styll continueth. And whyle they are moued from the West to mydnyght, because they are then moued by the quarter of the nyght flowyng, the nyght flowyng is agayne continuall. And whyle they are moued from mydnyght to the East, because they are then moued by the nyght quarter of reflowyng, the nyght reflowyng is agayne continuall. And thus twyse in the naturall day is the flowyng or increase, and twyse the reflowyng or decrease of the water of the sea. *The Sunne & Moone beyng in coniunction, what effectes they haue in moouyng the water of the sea.*

Ebbyng and flowyng twise in the naturall day.

B iii

Of flowyng.

It is agayne secondarylye to be knowen, that when the Moone after her coniunction with the Sunne, by her proper motion is departed from the Sunne towarde the East, accordyng to the order of the signes, goeyng towarde her fyrste quadrature with the Sunne (whiche the Uenetian Pilottes call, *il Quartirone*) euer before the Moone by her proper motion, come to that first quarter, whiche is the distaunce of the Moone from the Sunne towarde the East, accordyng to the order of the signes, by a quarter or fourth part of heauen, when the Sunne is so muche aboue the Horizon of the East parte in quarter of the day flowyng, howe muche the Moone is vnder the Horizon of the same parte of the East in the quarter of the nyght reflowyng, because then the Sunne is so muche distant from the strong poynt of the flowyng aboue the Horizon, as the Moone is distant from the strong poynt of the reflowyng vnder the Horizon, they are equipollent and of equall vertue, therefore then is neyther flowyng nor reflowyng of the water of the sea, but the water seemeth to stande: And then the Uenetians saye, *L'aqua è stanca*. But when the Sunne by the motion of the first moueable, commeth neare to the strong poynt of flowyng, whiche is aboue the Horizon in the day quarter of the flowyng, the Moone by the same motion of the first moueable, departeth so muche from the strong poynt of the reflowyng, whiche is vnder the Horizon in the nyght quarter of reflowyng, commyng towarde the weake poynt of the East flowyng: And then because the Sunne is nearer to the strong poynt of flowyng, whiche is aboue the Horizon in the day quarter of flowyng, then is the Moone in the strong poynt of reflowyng, whiche is vnder the Horizon in the nyght quarter of the reflowyng, the reflowyng is weakened, and the flowyng is fortifyed: and then the water of the sea begynneth to flowe. And howe muche more the Sunne approcheth to the strong poynt of the flowing, whiche is aboue the Horizon in the day quarter of the flowyng, so much more the Moone is departed from the strong poynt of the reflowyng, whiche is vnder the Horizon in the nyght quarter of the reflowyng, approchyng to the weake poynt of the East flowyng, and therefore the flowyng continueth. But when the Sunne

A quarter of heauē is three signes.

A tyme wherin is neyther ebbyng nor flowyng.

and reflowyng.

Sunne by motion of the first moueable, commeth to the strong poynt of the flowyng, whiche is aboue the Horizon in the day quarter of the flowyng, then the Moone is departed from the strong poynt of the reflowyng, whiche is vnder the Horizon in the nyght quarter of reflowyng, and is made neare to the weake poynt of the East flowyng, and therefore the flowyng yet continueth: But when the Moone shall come to the weake poynt of the East flowyng, shee then to the mouyng of the first moueable, is moued by the day quarter of flowyng, approchyng to the strong poynt of flowyng, whiche is aboue the Horizon: And the Sunne, because it is distant from the Moone lesse then a quarter, shall lykewyse be moued by the same day quarter of flowyng, approchyng to the weake poynt of the South reflowyng: And therefore because both are moued by the day quarter of the flowyng, the flowyng shall continue. And when the Sunne by the moouing of the fyrst moueable, commeth to the weake poynt of the South reflowyng, because then the Moone is nearer to the strong poynt of the flowyng, whiche is aboue the Horizon, then the Sunne to the strong poynt of the reflowyng, whiche is aboue the Horizon in the day quarter of the reflowyng, the flowyng shall continue. And when the Moone shall come to the strong poynt of the flowyng in the daye quarter of flowyng, the Sunne shall not yet be in the strong poynt of the reflowyng in the day quarter of the reflowing, because that the Sunne is distant from the Moone lesse then a quarter, but wyll come to it: and then the Moone shall depart from the strong poynt of the flowyng, and shalbe lesse distant from it then the sunne from the strong poynt of reflowyng: and therefore the flowyng shall yet continue, vntyll the sunne be so muche beyonde the South toward the West in the day quarter of reflowyng, howe much the moone on this syde the South towarde the East in the day quarter of the flowyng: And then the sunne shalbe so muche distant from the strong poynt of the reflowyng whiche is aboue the Horizon, beyonde the South in the day quarter of the reflowyng, howe muche the moone from the strong poynt of the flowyng, whiche is aboue the Horizon, before the South in the day quarter of flowyng: And incontinent, the Sunne and the moone shalbe equipollent or of equall strength, & therfore shalbe no flowing nor reflowing, as we haue sayd before. And when he sunne by the motion of the fyrst moueable, shall come to the strong point of reflowing in ye day quarter of reflowyng, the moone by the same motion of the fyrst moueable, shalbe departed so muche from the strong poynt of flowyng in the day quarter of flowyng, commyng towarde the weake poynt of the South reflowing: and then the moone shalbe more distant from the strong poynt of flowyng, then the sunne from the strong poynt of reflowyng: And so the sunne shalbe stronger then the moone, and therefore then shall begynne the reflowyng, and shall continue accordyng that the sunne shall approch to the strong poynt of the reflowyng, in the day quarter of reflowyng: and the moone shalbe departed from the strong poynt of the flowyng in the quarter of the day flowyng. And when the sonne shal come to the strong poynt of the reflowing, the moone shalbe departed from the strong poynt of the flowyng, and therefore the reflowyng shall yet continue. And when the moone shall come to the weake poynt of the South reflowyng, the sunne shalbe departed from the strong poynt of the reflowyng, in the day quarter of the reflowyng, commyng toward the weake poynt of the West flowyng: Yet shall the sunne be lesse distant from the strong poynt of the reflowyng, then the moone from the strong poynt of the flowyng, and therefore the reflowyng shall yet continue. And when the sunne shall come to the weake poynt of the West flowyng, the moone shalbe neare to the strong poynt of reflowyng, which is aboue the Horizon in the day quarter of reflowyng, and shalbe lesse distant from it, then the sunne from the strong poynt of the flowyng, whiche is under the Horizon in the nyght quarter of flowyng, because she is distant from the sunne lesse then a quarter or fourth part of heauen: therefore the reflowyng shall yet continue, untyll the sunne shalbe so much under the Horizon on the West part in the quarter of the nyght flowyng, howe muche the moone is aboue the Horizon on the same part of the West in the day quarter of reflowyng. And because

then

then the Sunne shalbe so much distaunt from the strong poynt of the flowyng, whiche is vnder the Horizon on the Weast parte, in the nyght quarter of flowyng, as the Moone from the strong poynt of reflowyng, whiche is aboue the Horizon, on that parte of the Weast in the day quarter of reflowyng: then the Sunne and the Moone shalbe equipollent (that is) of equal strength and vertue, and so shal there be neyther flowyng nor reflowyng. But when the Sunne, by the moouyng of the fyrst mooueable, shall come to the strong poynt of the flowyng, whiche is vnder the Horizon in the nyght quarter of the flowyng, the Moone by the same moouyng of the fyrst mooueable, shalbe departed as much from the strong poynt of reflowyng, whiche is aboue the Horizon in the day quarter of reflowyng: And then the Sunne shalbe lesse distaunt from the strong poynt of flowyng, in the nyght quarter of the flowyng, then the Moone from the strong poynt of reflowyng, in the day quarter of reflowyng, and therfore the Sunne shalbe stronger then the Moone: and then agayne shall begynne the flowyng, and shall continue (as is sayde before) vntyll the Sunne be so muche beyonde mydnyght towarde the East, in the nyght quarter of reflowyng, howe much the Moone on this syde mydnyght, toward the Weast, in the nyght quarter of flowyng, and then the Sunne shalbe so muche distaunt from the strong poynt of the reflowyng, as the Moone from the strong poynt of the flowyng: and then incontinent the Sunne and the Moone shalbe of equal strength, and there shalbe nother flowyng nor reflowyng. But when the Sunne, by the moouyng of the fyrst mooueable, commeth to the strong poynt of the reflowyng, in the nyght quarter of reflowyng, the Moone by the same moouyng of the fyrst mooueable, goeth backe, & is departed as muche from the strong poynt of the flowyng, in the night quarter of the flowyng, comming to ye weake poynt of midnight reflowyng: And then the Sunne shalbe lesse distaunt from the strong poynt of the reflowyng, in the nyght quarter of the flowyng, then the Moone from the strong poynt of flowyng in the nyght quarter of flowyng: and then shal the flowyng be weakened, and the reflowyng strengthened, and the water of the sea shall then agayne begyn to reflowe, whiche reflowyng shal continue

Of flowyng,

tinue (as is sayde before) vntyll the Sunne be so muche aboue the Horizon on the East parte, howe muche the Moone vnder the Horizon on the same parte of the East: And then the Sunne shalbe so muche distaunt from the strong poynt of the flowyng, whiche is aboue the Horizon, in the day quarter of the flowyng, howe much the Moone from the strong poynt of the reflowing, whiche is vnder the Horizon in the nyght quarter of the reflowyng: and then the Sunne and Moone agayne shalbe of equall strength, and there shalbe nother flowyng nor reflowyng. Then daylye (that is to say, in euery naturall day) shall returne the lyke change to this aforesaid, vntil the Moone by her proper motion, shall come to her fyrste quadrature with the Sunne, which the Pilottes or Mariners Venetians, cal *il Quartirone*, as I haue sayde before.

The Moone being in quartile aspect, or at the fyrste with the quarter, somewhat effectes it causeth in ebbyng and flowyng.

And when the Moone shall come to her fyrste quadrature with the Sunne, then when the Sunne shalbe in the weake poynt of the East for the flowyng, the Moone shalbe in the weake poynt of mydnyght, for the reflowyng: and then the Sunne shalbe so muche distaunt from the strong poynt of the flowyng, which is aboue the Horizon, on the East parte, in the day quarter of the flowyng, howe muche the Moone from the strong poynt of reflowyng, which is vnder the Horizon of the same part of the East, in the nyght quarter of the reflowyng: and so the Sunne and the Moone agayne shalbe of equall force and power, and there shalbe nother flowyng nor reflowyng notable, but onely smal, encreasyng and diminishyng.

A very litle ebbyng or flowyng.

And when the Sunne by the motion of the fyrst mooueable, shal come to the strong poynt of the flowyng, whiche is aboue the Horizon, on the East part, in the day quarter of the flowing, the Moone by the same motion of the fyrste mooueable, shall come lykewyse so muche to the strong poynt of the reflowyng, whiche is vnder the Horizon on the same parte of the East, in the night quarter of the reflowyng: and continually to the diurnall or day motion, the Sunne shalbe distauntiso muche from the strong poynt of flowyng, whiche is aboue the Horizon, in the day quarter of the flowyng, howe muche the Moone from the strong poynt of reflowyng, whiche is vnder the Horizon, in the nyght quarter of the reflowyng, and continentlye the Sunne and
Moone

and reflowyng.

Moone shalbe agayne of equall power, vntyl the Sunne by the mooupng of the fyrst mooueable, shal come to the strong poynt of flowyng, whiche is aboue the Horizon: And then lykewyse the Moone shal come to the strong poynt of reflowyng, whiche is vnder the Horizon, because these poyntes are distaunt one from the other by a quarter of heauen, as the Sunne and Moone are distaunt from them selues by a quarter of he. And when the Sunne by the motion of the fyrste mooueable, shall departe from the strong poynt of the flowyng, whiche is aboue the Horizon in the day quarter of the flowyng, commyng towarde the weake poynt of the South, reflowyng, the Moone by the same motion of the fyrste mooueable, shall lykewyse departe as muche from the strong poynt of the reflowyng, whiche is vnder the Horizon, commyng towarde the weake poynt of the East flowyng, and the Sunne shalbe contynually distaunt so muche from the strong poynt of flowyng, whiche is aboue the Horizon, howe much the Moone from the strong poynt of reflowyng, whiche is vnder the Horizon, vntyll the same come to the weake poynt of the South reflowyng: and then the Moone lykewyse shall come to the weake poynt of the East flowyng. And the Sunne and the Moone in all this tyme shalbe of equall strength, and incontinently shalbe nother flowyng nor reflowyng notable, and shalbe after the same manner whyle the Sunne to the motion of the fyrste mooueable, shalbe moued from the South to the Weast, because then the Moone by the same motion of the fyrste mooueable, shalbe moued from the East to the South: And lykewyse, whyle the Sunne shalbe moued from the Weast, to mydnyght, because then the Moone shalbe moued from the South, to the Weast: And lykewyse, whyle the Sunne shalbe moued from mydnyght to the East, because the Moone shal be moued from the Weast to mydnyght. And so in all the tyme of one reuolution of heauen, whiche is one daye naturall of foure and twentie houres, the sea shall neyther flowe nor reflowe sensiblye, but shall seeme to stande, because the Sunne and the Moone in all the tyme of that reuolu-

Eyght daies after the change, for the space of. 24. houres, is neyther ebbyng nor flowyng sensible.

Of flowyng,

reuolution of heauen, shalbe euer of equall power, without any notable difference. And this chaunceth about the eight day after the coniunction of the Moone with the Sunne. And this false quietnesse of the water of the sea, the Uenetians cal *Acqua de fele,* and vse this manner of saying, *Da gli otto, à i noue, L'acqua non si moue.* From the eyght day to the nienth, the water mooueth not.

When the Moone shalbe departed from the Sunne, beyond the fyrst quadrature, goyng towarde her opposition with the Sunne, then euer vntyll the Moone shall come vnto her opposition with the Sunne, when the Sunne shalbe so muche aboue the Horizon on the East part, in the day quarter of the flowyng, how much the Moone is vnder the Horizon on the same part of the East, in the nyght quarter of the reflowyng, the Sunne shalbe so muche distaunt from the strong poynt of the flowyng, whiche is aboue the Horizon, in the day quarter of flowyng, departyng from it by the motion of the fyrst mooueable, and commyng to the weake poynt of the reflowyng, howe muche the Moone from the strong poynt of the reflowyng, whiche is vnder the Horizon, in the nyght quarter of the reflowyng, commyng to it by the same motion of the fyrste mooueable: And then the Sunne and Moone shalbe agayne of equal power, and there shalbe neyther flowyng nor reflowyng. And when the Sunne by motion of the fyrst mooueable, shal come to the weake poynt of the South reflowyng, the Moone by the same motion of the fyrst mooueable, shall approche or come neare as muche to the strong poynt of the reflowyng, whiche is vnder the Horizon, in the nyght quarter of the reflowyng: and then the Moone shalbe nearer to the strong poynt of the reflowyng, whiche is vnder the Horizon, in the nyght quarter of the reflowyng, then the Sunne to the strong poynt of the flowyng, whiche is aboue the Horizon, in the day quarter of flowyng, because the Moone shalbe stronger then the Sunne: And accordyng that the Sunne by the motion of the fyrst mooueable, shal approch to the weake poynt of the South reflowyng, the Moone by the same motion of the fyrst mooueable, shal approch as much to the strong poynt of the reflowyng, whiche is vnder the Horizon. And so the

and reflowyng.

reflowyng shall continue vntyll the Sunne come to the weake poynt of the South reflowyng. And when the Sunne by the motion of the fyrste mooueable, shall departe from the weake poynt of the South reflowyng, and shalbe mooued by the day quarter of the reflowyng, approchyng to the strong poynt of the reflowyng, the Moone by the same motion of the fyrste mooueable, shall departe as muche from the strong poynt of the reflowyng, whiche is vnder the Horizon, in the nyght quarter of the reflowyng, and she shalbe also mooued by the quarter of reflowyng, as the Sunne conmyng to the weake poynt of the East flowyng, because the Sunne and the Moone are distaunt betweene them selues more then by a quarter of heauen: And so both shalbe mooued by the quarters of reflowyng, and therfore the reflowyng shall continue, vntyll the Sunne shalbe so muche beyonde the South, towarde the Weast, in the day quarter of the reflowyng, howe muche the Moone on this syde the South, towarde the East, in the day quarter of the flowyng. And then the Sunne shalbe so muche distaunt in the strong poynt of reflowyng, in the day quarter of reflowyng, departyng from it by the motion of the fyrste mooueable, towarde the Weast, howe muche the Moone from the strong poynt of flowyng, whiche is aboue the Horizon, in the day quarter of the flowyng, commyng to it: And so the Sunne and the Moone shalbe of equall force, and then shalbe neyther flowyng nor reflowyng. And when the Sunne by the motion of the fyrste mooueable, shalbe departed from the strong poynt of the reflowyng, which is aboue the Horizon, in the day quarter of the flowyng, commyng to the weake poynt of the Weast flowyng, the Moone by the same mouing of the fyrst mooueable, shall approch as much to the strong poynt of the flowyng, whiche is aboue the Horizon, in the day quarter of the flowyng, and then the Moone shalbe nearer to the strong poynt of the flowyng, in the day quarter of the flowyng, then the Sunne to the strong poynt of the reflowyng, in the day quarter of the reflowyng: and so the Moone shalbe stronger then the Sunne, and then shal begynne the flowyng. And as the Sunne shal cōtinually be departed from the strong poynt of reflowyng, in the day quarter of the reflowyng, so the Moone continually

shal

Of flowyng.

shal approche to the strong poynt of flowyng, in the day quarter of the flowyng, and so the flowyng shall continue. And when the Sunne shal come to the weake poynt of the Weast flowing, the Moone shall yet moue by the day quarter of the flowyng, because the Sunne and the Moone are distaunt one from the other more then by a quarter of heauen: and then the Moone shalbe nearer to the strong poynt of flowyng, in the quarter of the day flowing, then the Sunne to the strong poynt of flowing, whiche is vnder the Horizon, in the nyght quarter of the flowyng, and therefore the flowyng shall continue. And when the Moone shall come to the weake poynt of the South reflowyng, the Sunne shall passe the weake poynt of the Weast flowyng, approchyng to the strong poynt of the flowyng, whiche is vnder the Horizon, in the nyght quarter of the flowyng, and then the Sunne shalbe nearer the strong poynt of the flowyng, which is vnder the Horizon, in the night quarter of the flowyng, then the Moone to the strong poynt of the reflowyng, which is aboue the Horizon, in the day quarter of the reflowyng, and so the Sunne shalbe stronger then the Moone, and therefore the flowyng shall continue. And when the Sunne shall come to the strong poynt of flowyng, whiche is vnder the Horizon, in the nyght quarter of the flowyng, the Moone shall not yet be in the strong poynt of the reflowyng, whiche is aboue the Horizon, in the day quarter of the reflowyng, because the Moone is distaunt from the Sunne more then by a quarter of heauen, and therefore the flowyng shall yet continue, vntyl the Sunne be so muche vnder the Horizon on the Weast parte, in the nyght quarter of the flowyng, howe muche the Moone aboue the Horizon on the same parte of the Weast, in the day quarter of the reflowyng: and then the Sunne shalbe so muche distaunt from the strong poynt of the flowyng, whiche is vnder the Horizon in the nyght quarter of the flowyng, commyng to the weake poynt of midnight reflowyng, howe much the Moone from the strong poynt of reflowyng, whiche is aboue the Horizon, in the day quarter of the reflowyng commyng to it: and therefore the Sunne and the Moone shalbe of equal strength, and then shalbe neyther flowyng nor reflowyng. Afterwarde, when the Sunne

A long tyme of flowyng.

by

and reflowyng.

by the motion of the fyrste mooueable, shalbe distaunt from the strong poynt of the flowyng, whiche is vnder the Horizon on the Weast parte, in the nyght quarter of the flowyng, commyng towarde the weake poynt of mydnyght reflowyng, the Moone by the same motion of the fyrste mooueable, shall approche as muche to the strong poynt of reflowyng, whiche is aboue the Horizon, in the day quarter of the reflowyng commyng to it. And so the Moone shalbe nearer to the strong poynt of reflowyng, then the Sunne to the strong poynt of flowyng, and therfore the flowyng shall begynne, and shall continue in maner (as is sayde) vntyll the Sunne be so muche beyonde mydnyght, toward the East, in the nyght quarter of reflowyng, howe much the Moone before mydnyght towarde the Weast, in the nyght quarter of flowyng: and then the Sunne shalbe so much distaunt from the strong poynt of reflowyng, in the nyght quarter of reflowyng, goyng backwarde from it towarde the foresayde weake poynt of the East flowyng, howe muche the Moone from the poynt of the strong flowyng, in the nyght quarter of the flowyng commyng to it: and then the Sunne and the Moone shalbe of equall force, and there shalbe neyther flowyng nor reflowyng. And when the Sunne by the motion of the fyrst mooueable, shalbe departed from the strong poynt of reflowyng, vnder the Horizon, which is in the nyght quarter of reflowyng, commyng towarde the weake poynt of the East flowyng, the Moone by the same motion of the fyrst mooueable, shal approch as much to the strong poynt of flowyng, which also is vnder the Horizon, in the nyght quarter of the flowyng commyng to it. And because then the Moone is nearer to the strong poynt of flowyng, whiche is in the nyght quarter of flowyng, then the Sunne to the strong poynt of reflowyng, whiche is in the nyght quarter of reflowyng: then shall the flowyng begynne and continue in manner aforesayde, vntyll the Sunne be so muche aboue the Horizon on the East parte, in the day quarter of flowyng, howe muche the Moone vnder the Horizon, on the same parte of the East, in the nyght quarter of reflowyng. And because the Sunne shalbe so much distaunt from the strong poynt of flowyng, whiche is aboue the Horizon,

Offlowyng,

in the day quarter of flowyng, commyng by the motion of the fyrst mooueable, towarde the weake poynt of the South reflowyng, howe muche the Moone from the strong poynt of reflowyng, whiche is vnder the Horizon, in the nyght quarter of reflowyng, commyng by the same motion of the fyrst mooueable towarde it, they shalbe of equall force, and so shalbe neyther flowyng nor reflowyng. And in this maner, the flowyng and reflowyng shall continue in euery naturall day, vntyll the Moone shall come to her opposition with the Sunne.

The Moone being in opposition with the Sunne, what effectes they haue in moouyng the water of the sea.

And when the Moone shall come to her opposition with the Sunne, then when the Sunne shalbe in the weake poynt of the East flowyng, the Moone shal lykewyse be in the weake poynt of the West flowyng: and then shal the flowyng begyn, and shall continue as long as the Sunne shalbe mooued to the moouyng of the fyrste mooueable, from the weake poynt of the East flowyng, by the day quarter of the flowyng, to the weake poynt of the South reflowyng. And the Moone then in al this tyme, shalbe mooued lykewyse to the moouyng of the fyrste mooueable, from the weake poynt of the West flowyng, by the nyght quarter of flowyng, to the weake poynt of mydnyght reflowyng: and then the flowyng shall ceasse, and the reflowyng begynne, and continue as long as the Sunne at the moouyng of the fyrste mooueable, shalbe mooued from the weake poynt of the South reflowyng, by the day quarter of reflowyng, vnto the weake poynt of the West flowyng, and the Moone in all that tyme shalbe mooued lykewyse to the moouyng of the fyrste mooueable, from the weake poynt of mydnyght reflowyng, by the nyght quarter of reflowyng, vnto the weake poynt of the East flowyng: and then the reflowyng shall ceasse, and the flowyng shall begynne agayne, and shall continue as long as the Sunne shalbe mooued to the motion of the fyrste mooucable, from the weake poynt of the West flowyng, by the nyght quarter of the flowyng, vnto the weake poynt of mydnyght reflowyng. And then the Moone in al that time, by the same moouyng of the fyrst mooueable, shall lykewyse be mooued from the weake poynt of the East flowyng, by the day quarter of the flowyng, vnto the weake poynt of reflowyng: and then the flowyng shal

and reflowyng.

shall ceasse, and the reflowyng begyn, and shall continue as long as the Sunne, by the mouyng of the first moueable, shalbe moued from the weake poynt of mydnyght reflowyng, by the night quarter of the reflowyng vnto the weake poynt of the East flowyng. And then the Moone in all this tyme by the same motion of the fyrste moueable, shalbe moued lykewyse from the weake poynt of the South reflowyng, by the day quarter of the reflowyng, vnto the weake poynt of the West flowyng: and then the reflowyng shall ceasse.

And when the Moone shall passe her opposition with the Sunne by her proper motion, goyng to her seconde quadrature with the Sunne, then when the Moone shalbe so muche aboue the Horizon on the East part in the day quarter of flowyng, how muche the Sunne vnder the Horizon on the same part of the East in the nyght quarter of the reflowyng, because then the Moone shalbe so much distant from the strong poynt of flowing whiche is aboue the Horizon in the day quarter of flowyng, how muche the Sunne from the strong poynt of reflowyng, whiche is vnder the Horizon on the same parte of the East in the nyght quarter of reflowyng, then the Sunne and the Moone shalbe of equall power, and therfore shalbe neyther flowyng nor reflowyng. And when the Moone by motion of the fyrste moueable, shalbe departed from the strong poynt of flowyng, which is aboue the Horizon in the day quarter of flowyng, commyng towarde the weake poynt of the South reflowyng, the Sunne by the same motion of the fyrste moueable, shall approche as muche to the strong poynt of reflowyng, whiche is vnder the Horizon of the nyght quarter of reflowyng, commyng to it: and then because the Sunne shalbe lesse distant from the strong poynt of reflowyng, whiche is vnder the Horizon on the East parte in the nyght quarter of reflowyng, then the Moone from the strong poynt of flowyng, whiche is aboue the Horizon on the same parte of the East in the day quarter of flowyng, the reflowyng shall beginne and continue. And when the Moone by the motion of the firste moueable, shall come to the weake poynt of the South reflowyng, the Sunne shall yet be vnder the Horizon in the nyght quarter of reflowyng, because the Sunne

The Moone past her opposition with the Sunne, what effectes they cause in mouyng the water of the sea.

C i and

Of flowyng,

and the Moone are distant frō them selues more then by a quarter of heauen, and then the Moone to the mouyng of the firste moueable, shalbe moued by the day quarter of reflowyng, as also the Sunne in lyke maner by the nyght quarter of reflowyng, commyng to the strong poynt of reflowyng in the day quarter of reflowyng, and so the reflowyng shall continue. And when the Moone shall approche to the strong poynt of reflowyng in the day quarter of reflowyng, the Sunne shall approche to the weake poynt of the East flowyng, in the nyght quarter of reflowyng, and shalbe further distant from the strong poynt of flowyng, whiche is aboue the Horizon, in the day quarter of flowyng, then the Moone from the strong poynt of the reflowyng, whiche is lykewyse aboue the Horizon in the day quarter of reflowyng: and so the reflowyng shall continue, vntyll the Moone be so muche beyonde the South towarde the West in the day quarter of the reflowyng, as the Sunne before the South towarde the East in the day quarter of flowyng: and then the Moone shalbe so farre distant from the strong poynt of reflowyng in the day quarter of reflowyng, howe muche the Sunne from the strong poynt of flowyng in the day quarter of flowyng: and so the Sunne and the Moone shalbe of equall force, and there shalbe neyther flowyng nor reflowyng. And when the Moone by the motion of the firste moueable, shall depart from the strong poynt of reflowyng, commyng towarde the weake poynt of the West reflowyng, the Sunne by the same motion of the firste moueable, shall approche as muche to the strong poynt of flowyng, in the day quarter of flowyng: And then because the Sunne shalbe nearer to the strong poynt of flowyng, whiche is in the day quarter of flowyng, then the Moone in the strong poynt of reflowyng, whiche is in the day quarter of reflowyng, the flowyng shall begynne and continue accordyng that the Moone, to the mouyng of the fyrste moueable, shalbe departed from the strong poynt of reflowyng, in the day quarter of reflowyng, commyng towarde the weake poynt of the West flowyng: and the Sunne shall approche to the strong poynt of the flowyng, in the day quarter of the flowyng commyng to it.

and reflowyng.

And when the Moone to the mouyng of the fyrste moueable, shall come to the weake poynt of the West flowyng, the Sunne yet by the same motion of the first moueable, shall moue by the day quarter of the flowyng, becauſe the Sunne and Moone are diſtant the one from the other more then by a quarter of heauen: & the Sunne ſhalbe more neare to the ſtrõg poynt of the flowyng, in the day quarter of flowyng, then the Moone to the ſtrong poynt of reflowyng, in the day quarter of reflowyng, and therefore the flowyng ſhall continue. And when the Sunne ſhal come to the weake poynt of the South reflowyng, ẏ Moone ſhalbe vnder the Horizon on the West part in the nyght quarter of the flowyng, and ſhalbe nearer to the ſtrong poynt of the flowyng, whiche is vnder the Horizon in the nyght quarter of the flowyng, then the Sunne to the ſtrong poynt of reflowyng, whiche is aboue the Horizon in the day quarter of reflowyng: And therefore the flowyng ſhall yet continue, vntyll the Moone be ſo muche vnder the Horizon on the West parte, in the nyght quarter of the flowyng, howe muche the Sunne aboue the Horizon on the ſame part of the West in the day quarter of the reflowyng. And then the Moone ſhalbe ſo muche diſtant from the ſtrong poynt of flowyng, vnder the Horizon in the nyght quarter of flowyng, commyng towarde the weake poynt of mydnyght reflowyng, howe muche the Sunne from the ſtrong poynt of reflowyng aboue the Horizon, in the day quarter of reflowyng commyng to it: and ſo the Sunne and Moone ſhalbe of equall ſtrength, and then ſhalbe neyther flowyng nor reflowyng. And when the Moone by the motion of the fyrſte moueable, ſhall departe from the ſtrong poynt of flowyng vnder the Horizon, in the nyght quarter of flowyng, commyng towarde the weake poynt of mydnyght reflowyng, the Sunne by the ſame motion of the firſte moueable, ſhall approche as muche to the ſtrong poynt of reflowyng, whiche is aboue the Horizon, in the day quarter of reflowyng commyng to it: And then the Sunne ſhalbe nearer to the ſtrong poynt of reflowyng, whiche is aboue the Horizon, in the day quarter of reflowyng, then the Moone to the ſtrong poynt of flowyng, whiche is vnder the Horizon, in the nyght quarter of flowyng.

Of flowyng,

And therefore then shall begynne the reflowyng, and shal continue accordyng that the Moone shall departe from the strong poynt of flowyng, whiche is vnder the Horizon in the nyght quarter of flowyng, approchyng vnto the weake poynt of mydnyght reflowyng, and the Sunne shall approche to the strong poynt of reflowing, which is aboue the Horizon in the day quarter of reflowyng. And when the Moone by the motion of the first moueable, shall come to the weake poynt of mydnyght reflowyng, the Sunne shal yet be aboue the Horizon on the West part in the day quarter of reflowyng, commyng by the motion of the first moueable, to the weake poynt of the West flowyng, because the Sunne and the Moone are distant one from the other more then by a quarter: And then the Sunne shalbe more distant from the strong poynt of flowyng, whiche is vnder the Horizon on the West part in the quarter of the nyght flowyng, then the Moone from the strong poynt of reflowyng, which also is vnder the Horizon on the part of the East in the night quarter of reflowyng. And therefore the reflowyng shall continue vntyll the Moone be so muche beyonde mydnyght towarde the East, how much the Sunne before mydnyght towarde the West: and then the Moone shalbe so farre distant from the strong poynt of reflowyng in the nyght quarter of reflowyng, goyng from it by the motion of the firste moueable, and commyng to the weake poynt of the East flowyng, howe muche the Sunne from the poynt of flowyng in the nyght quarter of flowyng, commyng to it by the same motion of the firste moueable: and so the Sunne and the Moone shalbe of equall force, and then shalbe neyther flowyng nor reflowyng. And when the Moone by the motion of the first moueable, shalbe departed from the strong poynt of reflowyng, whiche is vnder the Horizon, on the East parte of the nyght quarter of reflowing toward the weake poynt of the East flowyng, the Sunne by the same mouyng of the fyrst moueable, shall approche as muche to the strong poynt of flowyng, whiche is vnder the Horizon on the West part in the nyght quarter of flowyng commyng to it: And then because the Moone shalbe more distant frō the strong poynt of reflowyng, then the Sunne from the strong poynt of flowyng, then shal begyn the flowyng,

becauſe

and reflowyng.

because the Sunne shalbe stronger then the Moone. And howe muche more the Moone shalbe distant from the strong poynt of reflowyng, in the nyght quarter of reflowyng, so much more the Sunne shall approch to the strong poynt of flowing, in the night quarter of flowyng, and so the flowyng shall continue: and when the Moone shall come to the weake poynt of the East flowyng, the Sunne shall yet be in the nyght quarter of flowyng, because the Sunne is distant from the Moone more then by a quarter of heauen, and the Sunne shalbe nearer to the strong point of flowing in the night quarter of flowing, then the Moone to the strong poynt of reflowyng, which is in the night quarter of reflowing: and so the flowing shal yet continue vntyl the Moone be so much aboue the Horizon on the East parte, howe muche the Sunne vnder the Horizon on the same parte of the East: And then the Moone shal so much be distant from the strong point of flowing, whiche is aboue the Horizon in the day quarter of flowyng, departyng from it by the motion of the first moueable towarde the weake poynt of the South reflowyng, howe muche the Sunne from the strong poynt of reflowyng, which is vnder the Horizon in the night quarter of reflowyng, commyng to it by the same motion of the first moueable. And then the Sunne & the Moone shalbe of equall force, and there shalbe neyther flowyng nor reflowyng, and the first disposition shall returne agayne, and suche flowyng and reflowyng, shall continue euery natural day in this maner, vntyll the Moone shall come to her quadrature with the Sunne.

And when the Moone shalbe in the seconde quadrature, then the water of the sea, shall neyther flowe nor reflowe, but shall seeme to be at rest as it was in the first quadrature, in the which, in the whole reuolution of heauen, the Sunne and the Moone were euer of equall strength for the causes there declared: for the same are the causes of the seconde quadrature, which are also of the fyrst, and is about. 21. dayes. And this quietnes or stay of the water of the sea (as is sayde before) the Uenetians call *Acqua de sele*, and vse this saying: *Da vent'uno a venti due, l'acqua non va ne su, ne giu.* From the. 21. to. 22. the water goeth neyther vp nor downe.

The Moone beyng in the last quarter, causeth the same effectes as in the first.

C iii   And

Of flowyng,

And when the Moone by her proper motion shall passe this seconde quadrature, proceedyng to her coniunction with the Sunne, then the Moone shalbe distant from the Sunne, lesse then the fourth parte of heauen. And then when she shalbe so muche aboue the Horizon on the East parte, in the day quarter of flowyng, as the Sunne vnder the Horizon on the same parte of the East, in the nyght quarter of reflowyng, then the Moone shalbe so muche distant from the strong poynt of flowyng, which is aboue the Horizon, in ye day quarter of flowyng, commyng to it by the motion of the fyrste moueable, howe muche the Sunne from the strong poynt of reflowyng, whiche is vnder the Horizon in the nyght quarter of reflowing, going from it by the same motion of the fyrste moueable towarde the weake poynt of the East flowyng: and then the Sunne and the Moone shalbe of equall power, and there shalbe neyther flowyng nor reflowyng. And when the Moone by the motion of the fyrst moueable, shall come to the strong poynt of flowyng, whiche is aboue the Horizon in the day quarter of flowyng, the Sunne by the same motion of the first moueable, shall depart as muche from the strong poynt of reflowyng, whiche is vnder the Horizon in the nyght quarter of reflowyng, toward the weake poynt of the East flowyng. And then because the Moone shalbe lesse distant from the strong poynt of flowyng, whiche is aboue the Horizon, in the day quarter of flowyng, then the Sunne from the strong poynt of reflowyng, the Moone shalbe stronger then the Sunne, and therefore then shall begynne the flowyng: and howe much more the Moone shall approche to the strong poynt of flowyng, so muche more the Sunne shalbe distant from the strong poynt of reflowyng, approching to the weake poynt of the East flowing, and therefore the flowyng shall continue. And when the Sunne by the mouyng of the fyrste moueable, shall come to the weake poynt of the East flowyng, because the Moone shall yet be in the day quarter of flowyng, for that she is distant from the Sunne lesse then a fourth parte of heauen, she shalbe lesse distant from the strong poynt of flowyng, whiche is aboue the Horizon, in the day quarter of flowyng, then the Sunne from the strong poynt of reflowyng, whiche is vnder the Horizon, in the

nyght

nyght quarter of reflowyng, therefore the flowyng shall yet continue. And when the Moone shall come to the weake point of the South reflowyng, the Sunne shalbe aboue the Horizon, in the day quarter of flowyng, and shalbe nearer to the strong poynt of flowyng, then the Moone to the strong poynt of reflowyng, whiche is after mydday (or the South) in the day quarter of reflowyng, because the Sunne is distant from the Moone lesse then the fourth parte of heauen, and therefore the flowyng shall continue vntyll the Moone be so muche beyonde the South towarde the West, in the day quarter of reflowyng, howe muche the Sunne before the South towarde the East, in the day quarter of flowyng: And then the Moone shalbe so muche distant from the strong poynt of reflowyng, in the day quarter of reflowyng, commyng to it by the motion of the firste moueable, howe muche the Sunne from the strong poynt of flowyng, in the day quarter of flowyng, departyng from it by the same motion of the firste moueable: and so the Sunne and the Moone shalbe of equall force, and there shalbe neyther flowyng nor reflowyng. And when the Moone by the motion of the firste moueable, shal approch to the strong poynt of reflowyng, in the day quarter of reflowyng, the Sunne by the same motion of the first moueable, shall goe backe and depart as muche from the strong poynt of flowyng, in the day quarter of flowyng: and then the Moone shalbe nearer to the strong poynt of reflowyng, in the day quarter of reflowyng, then the Sunne to the strong poynt of flowyng, in the day quarter of flowyng: and so the Moone shalbe stronger then the Sunne, and therefore shall begynne the reflowyng: and the flowyng and reflowyng, shall continue in the same maner as is sayde.

When the Moone departeth from her coniunction with the Sunne, and is not come to her first quadrature with the Sunne, and is betwene the coniunction and fyrst quadrature, and when the Moone shall come to her coniunction with the Sunne, then agayne al the dispositiō before declared, shal returne in al poynts in lyke maner as is sayde. Therefore this motion of the water of the sea whereof we haue spoken, is a motion folowyng the motion of the Sunne & Moone to the motion of the first moueable.

A briefe collection of all the premisses.

C iiii   For

Of flowyng,

For yf you shall wel consyder that we haue sayde of the flowyng and reflowyng (that is) increase and decrease, or accesse and recesse of the water of the sea, you shall vnderstande that the begynnynges of suche flowyng and reflowyng, and lykewyse the rest and quietnesse, chaunce diuersly in the houres of the day and the nyght: For they come not euer in the same houres of the day, as is manifestly knowen to suche as obserue suche flowyng and reflowyng, or false rest or quietnesse of the water of the sea. And therefore by the aforesayde doeth appeare that the water of the sea hath motion of flowyng, once in the day, and once in the nyght: and lykewyse of reflowyng once in the day, and once in the nyght.

Ebbyng and flowyng begin not alwayes at one houre.

It is manifest also that the flowyng doth not begyn euer the same houre of the day or nyght, but at diuers houres: and lykewyse the reflowyng.

Also the tyme of flowyng or reflowyng, proceedeth inordinately when the Moone is in her quadratures with the Sunne, that is, in the first or seconde.

There chaunceth sometymes great increase of waters, sometyme lesse, sometymes meane, when the Moone shalbe in any other place from the sunne beside these foure: That is to meane, in the coniunction, or opposition, or her first quadrature, or second with the Sunne.

And as are sometymes increases of waters, greater, lesse, and meane, euen so are the decreases in lyke maner.

Great motions of the water in the coniunction of the Sunne and Moone.

The greatest concourses and motions of waters, are when the Moone is in coniunction with the Sunne, & also the greatest flowynges and reflowynges. Lykewyse in opposition of the Moone with the Sunne, and greater then in the tyme of the coniunction of the Moone with the sunne. For the superior bodyes, by their motion & light, geue their influence into these inferior bodyes. And so much more as they haue of lyght, so much more & stronglyer they worke and because in oppositiō of the Moone with the Sunne, the Moone is ful of light & her light is toward vs, therfore is it reasonable ÿ then should be caused greater flowynges and reflowyngs, then in her coniunction with the Sunne.

Greatest motions in opposition of the Sunne and Moone.

Neuertheleesse, because that in her coniunction with the Sunne, the

the Sunne & Moone are both vnite together, and their vertues, therfore also are great encreasynges and decreasynges of waters, because both their vertues are vnite, as I haue sayde, but yet greater in the opposition then in the coniunction, for causes before rehearsed.

The Moone beyng in her quadratures with the Sunne, the water of the sea hath no determinate tyme of flowyng or reflowing, and then are the lesse concourses of waters, & least flowing and reflowyng. And suche motion of the sea, the Uenetians call De sele: and then the water of the sea hath no determinate begynnyng of flowyng or reflowyng, but is mooued inordinately in dyuers maner, sometyme commyng, and sometyme goyng. The cause of this diuersitie is, because the Sunne & the Moone, where so euer they shalbe in mooupng to the water equally, or as it were equally, haue contrarietie in what so euer poynt they shalbe. For in what so euer poynt the Sunne shalbe, the Moone shalbe in the point of opposite vertue, contrary to the place of the Sunne, or neare. *Smal motions of the water without determinate time alwayes in the quadratures of the Sunne and Moone.*

And when the Moone shalbe without the sayde foure places, then the water of the sea shal begynne to come or goe. And when the Sunne and Moone shalbe in equall poyntes of vertue of the quarters of contrary operation, the concourses of waters shalbe so muche the greater, in howe much the Moone shalbe nearer to her coniunction with the Sunne, or to the opposition: and so much the lesse, in howe muche the Moone shalbe nearer to the quadratures, lykewyse also the flowynges and reflowynges shalbe so muche the greater. For yf the Moone shalbe betweene her coniunction with the Sunne and the fyrst quadrature, then the Moone to the moyyng of the fyrste moueable, doot) folowe the Sunne in his rysyng: and then shalbe the begynnyng of the day flowyng, of the day after the rysyng of the Sunne, about three of the clocke, or before: that is to meane, when the Sunne shalbe so muche aboue the Horizon on the part of the East, in the day quarter of flowyng, how muche the Moone vnder the Horizon on the same parte of the East, in the myght quarter of reflowyng, because then the Sunne & Moone shalbe of equall force, because they shalbe in the poyntes of equal *Note.*

The Moon foloweth the Sunne in rysing.

When flowyng shalbe three houres after Sunne rysing.

ver-

Offlowyng,

vertue in the quarters of contrary operation, and the begynnyng of the nyght flowyng shalbe in the nyght, after the fal of the Sunne (that is) when the Sunne shalbe so muche under the Horizon, on the same parte of the Weast, in the day quarter of flowyng, howe muche the Moone under the Horizon on the same parte of the Weast, in the day quarter of reflowyng: And the begynnyng of the day reflowyng shalbe in the day after noone, when the Sunne shalbe so muche after noone, in the day quarter of reflowyng, howe muche the Moone before noone, in the day quarter of flowyng: And the begynnyng of the reflowyng of the nyght, shalbe in the day after mydnyght (that is) when the Sunne shalbe so muche after the poynt of mydnyght, in the nyght quarter of reflowyng, howe muche the Moone before hym in the nyght quarter of flowyng. And yf the Moone be betweene the fyrste quadrature and the opposition, the Moone yet in her rysyng foloweth the Sunne, and then shalbe the begynnyng of the day flowyng, in the day after noone, about euenyng (that is) a litle before or after, that when the Sunne shalbe so muche aboue the Horizon on the parte of the Weast, in the day quarter of reflowyng, howe muche the Moone aboue the Horizon on the parte of the East, in the day quarter of flowyng, and the begynnyng of the nyght flowyng, shalbe in the day before day (that is) about mornyng, before or after (that is) when the Sunne shalbe so muche under the Horizon on the parte of the East, in the nyght quarter of reflowyng, howe muche the Moone under the Horizon on the parte of the Weast, in the nyght quarter of flowyng: and the begynnyng of the day reflowyng, shalbe in the day before noone, when the Sunne shalbe so muche before the poynt of noone, howe much the Moone after the poynt of mydnyght. And the begynnyng of the nyght reflowyng, shalbe in the nyght, before mydnyght, when the Sunne shalbe so muche before the poynt of mydnyght, in the quarter of the nyght flowyng, howe muche the Moone after the poynt of noone, or mydday, in the day quarter of reflowyng. And yf the Moone shalbe betweene the opposition of the Sunne, and her seconde quadrature with the Sunne, then the Moone in her rysyng

Ebbyng after noone.

and reflowyng.

rysyng, goeth before the Sunne, and then the begynnynges both of flowyng and reflowyng, be in lyke maner as they were when the Moone was betwene the coniunction and fyrst quadrature. For the begynnyng of the day flowyng, shalbe in the day about three of the clocke, before or after (that is) when the Sunne shalbe so muche aboue the Horizon on the East parte, in the day quarter of flowyng, howe muche the Moone aboue the Horizon on the West parte, in the day quarter of reflowyng. And the begynnyng of the nyght flowyng shalbe in the nyght, when the Sunne shalbe so muche vnder the Horizon on the part of the West, in the nyght quarter of flowyng, howe muche the Moone vnder the Horizon on the parte of the East, in the nyght quarter of reflowyng: But the begynnyng of the day reflowyng, shalbe in the day after noone, when the Sunne shalbe so muche after the poynt of the South, in the day quarter of reflowyng, as the Moone before the poynt of mydnyght, in the nyght quarter of flowyng. And the begynnyng of the nyght reflowyng, shalbe in the day, when the Sunne shalbe so muche after the poynt of mydnyght, in the nyght quarter of reflowyng, howe muche the Moone before the poynt of noone, in the day quarter of flowyng. And yf the Moone shalbe betwene the seconde quadrature, and her coniunction with the Sunne, then the Moone also in her rysyng shall goe before the Sunne: and then shalbe the begynnynges of flowyng and reflowyng in the same houres, as they be when the Moone is betwene the fyrst quadrature and opposition: because the begynning of the day flowyng, in the day after noone about euenyng, before or after, when the Sunne shalbe so muche aboue the Horizon on the part of the West, in the day quarter of reflowing, howe much the Moone vnder the Horizon on the same part of the West, in the nyght quarter of flowyng: and the beginning of the night flowing shalbe in the night, about mornyng, before or after, when the Sunne shalbe so muche vnder the Horizon on the parte of the East, in the nyght quarter of reflowyng, howe muche the Moone aboue the Horizon on the same parte of the East, in the day quarter of flowyng.

The Moone rysing before the Sunne.

Note.

But

Of flowyng.

But the begynnyng of the day reflowyng, shalbe in the day before noone, when the Moone shalbe so muche after the poynt of mydday, or the South, in the day quarter of reflowyng, howe muche the Sunne before it in the day quarter of flowyng, and the begynnyng of the nyght reflowyng shalbe in the nyght before mydnyght (that is) when the Moone shalbe so muche after the poynt of mydnyght, in the nyght quarter of reflowyng, howe much the Sunne before the poynt of mydnyght, in the nyght quarter of flowyng. And hereby it appeareth, that as wel the flowyng as reflowyng of the water of the sea, begyn not euer in the same houres of the day or nyght: for the begynnyng of flowyng is eyther in the begynnyng of the day, or begynnyng of the nyght, whiche chaunceth, the Moone beyng in coniunction or opposition to the Sunne: or is before day from the mornynges towarde the day, or from the day, vntyll foure of the clocke, or thereabout, or is before Euenyng, towarde Euentyde, and from thence to the Cocke crowyng, or thereabout: whiche chaunceth when the Moone is betweene her coniunction or opposition with the Sunne, or anye of the quadratures. The begynnyng of reflowyng is eyther at noone, or at mydnyght, as when the Moone is in coniunction or opposition with the Sunne, or is before noone, or after, or before mydnyght, or after, as when the Moone is betweene her coniunction or opposition with the Sunne, and anye of the quadratures. It is apparent also, that sometymes the water of the sea hath no determinate or certayne begynnyng, neyther order of flowyng or reflowyng, which chaunceth, the Moone beyng in her quadratures with the Sunne. It is manyfest also, that al flowyng of the water of the sea, is caused by respect to the Horizon, on the parte of the East or West. And euery reflowyng by respecte to the Meridian, or to the poynt of mydday, or mydnyght.

A general obseruation for the beginnyng of ebbyng and flowyng.

Note.

In what Horizon this discourse taketh place.

Here is also to be consydered, that all that is sayde, are moste certaynely true in a ryght Horizon, but in an oblique or syde Horizon, they sometymes fayle, as shalbe sayde hereafter folowyng.

and reflowyng.

It chaunceth (as I haue sayde) that the water of the sea doth sometime wander or decline from the order aboue prescribed, yet commonly, and for the moste parte keepeth that due order. Such maner of declynyng is after two sortes: For there is eyther disorder, or errrour, in the houre of the begynnyng of the motion of the flowyng or reflowyng, or in the myddest of the motion: that is to meane, that they haue greater or lesser courses then at other tymes, or otherwyse greater or lesser increases and decreases. The errour comming in the houre of motion, may come of three causes: As, by reason of the situation of the region, or by reason of the bodyes supercelestiall, or by change of the ayre. By reason of situation of regions, chaunceth diuersitie onely in the houre of the begynnyng of the flowyng, because the begynnyng thereof hath respecte to the Horizon, or is by respecte to the Horizon: for in the begynnyng of reflowyng is no diuersitie nor errour, because the begynnyng of the reflowyng, is by respecte to the Meridian circle. Agayne, by reason of the situation of the region, diuersitie chaunceth thus, that is, that eyther the region is vnder the Equinoctial circle, or without it. And if it be vnder the circle, because they haue a ryght Horizon, and the dayes be there euer equall with the nyghtes there, at all tymes of the yeere. That we haue sayde of diuers houres of the begynnyng of flowyng, is certaynely true: But regions distaunt from the Equinoctiall, because they haue a wyndyng or slope Horizon in them, the begynnynges of flowyng are as in regions vnder the Equinoctiall, onely in two tymes of the yeere: That is to say, in the Spryng tyme, or Equinoctial Uernal, and in the tyme of Autumne, or Equinoctiall Autumnall, that is to say, About the myddest of the Moneth of Marche, and about the myddest of the Moneth of September: But in other tymes of the yeere, or from the Uernal Equinoctial, by the whole Sommer, vntil the equinoctial Autumnal, it is otherwise, because the begynnyng of the day flowyng, yf the flowyng be before noone, that is, about the mornyng, it shalbe later then it ought to be: That is to say, more of the day then is in regions vnder the Equinoctiall, and that because, that in suche regions the day begynneth sooner, or the Sunne ryseth sooner, then in regions whiche

The beginning of flowyng is by respecte of the Horizon

The begynnyng of ebbyng, is by respecte of the Meridian circle.

Of flowyng,

whiche are vnder the Equinoctiall: for the declynyng of the oblique or syde Horizon (although these regions be vnder one and the same Meridian.) But and yf the begynnyng of the day flowyng be after noone, that is, about euenyng, then suche begynnyng shalbe sooner then it is in regions vnder the Equinoctial, (that is to say) in fewer houres of the day: because that then the Sunne falleth latelyer then in regions whiche be vnder the Equinoctial. But the begynnyng of the nyght flowyng, yf it be before mydnyght, it is sooner in the sayde places or regions (that is to say) in lesse tyme of the nyght, or in lesse tyme after the fal of the Sunne, then in regions vnder the Equinoctiall: because that then the nyght begynneth to them afterwarde. And yf the begynnyng of the nyght flowyng be after mydnyght (that is) towarde the day, it shalbe later (that is) of more houres, or more neare the day, then is in regions vnder the Equinoctiall: because the Sunne ryseth sooner to them, then to those that be vnder the Equinoctiall. And this diuersitie groweth so much, that sometyme it chaunceth to see two flowings in one day, and none in the nyght: whiche chaunceth for the inequalitie of the dayes, with their nyghtes. For in howe much the artificiall day shalbe longer then his nyght, so muche suche diuersitie and errour groweth more euidently. Therefore in the longest dayes of the yeere, suche diuersitie shall appeare manyfestly. But from the Equinoctiall Autumnal, by al Wynter, vntyl the Equinoctial Uernall, it is contrary: because the begynnlng of the day flowyng, yf it be before noone, that is, about the mornyng, then shal it be sooner then it shoulde be (that is to say) in fewer houres of the day, then it shoulde be in a ryght Horizon: for then the day begynneth latelyer, or the Sunne ryseth latelyer to them that haue a wyndyng or crooked Horizon. And yf such flowyng shalbe after noone (that is) about euenyng, then the begynnyng of suche flowyng shalbe later (that is) more towarde the euenyng, or nearer to the fallyng of the Sunne, then in regions which are vnder the Horizon: For in sayde or crooked Horizon, the nyght is sooner, and the Sunne falleth sooner then in a ryght Horizon. Also, the begynnyng of the nyght flowyng, yf it shalbe before mydnyght, it shalbe later and more in the nyght, then in regions

Two flowyngs in one day, and none in the nyght.

and reflowyng.

gions vnder the Equinoctial: because then the nyght shal sooner begynne in the crooked Horizon, then in the ryght, because the Sunne fyrste falleth in the crooked Horizon, then in the ryght. And yf the begynnyng of the nyght flowyng shalbe after mydnyght, that is, towarde the day, then suche begynnyng of flowyng in the crooked Horizon, shalbe sooner (that is) in fewer houres of the nyght (that is) more before the day, or before the rysyng of the Sunne, then shalbe in regions whiche be vnder the Equinoctiall: because the Sunne ryseth latelyer then in regions vnder the Equinoctiall. And suche diuersitie groweth so muche, that sometime shalbe two flowynges in the nyght, and none in the day: And this chaunceth for the inequalitie and encrease of the nyght aboue his day. For in howe muche the nyght shalbe longer then his day, so muche the more groweth suche diuersitie: and therfore suche diuersitie shall appeare greatest in the longest nyght of the yeere. Wherefore, by the aforesayde, it is manyfest, that howe much the nearer we shalbe to the Equinoctial, so muche the lesse shall appeare the diuersitie in the houre of the begynnyng of flowyng of the water: And how much the Sunne shalbe nearer vnto the standings or stayinges of the Sunne (called Solstitium) or the longest daies, & longest nightes, so much greater and more certaine shalbe the diuersitie, and shal appeare more manyfestly. Furthermore, diuersitie chaunceth by reason of the heauenly bodyes, and errour, not onely in the begynnings of flowyng, but also of reflowyng. *Note.*

For when anye of the great and luminous Starres (as are Venus and Iupiter) shalbe about the Sunne or Moone, they helpe them in moouyng the water of the sea: and therfore by this meanes also, they haue their due order. Lykewyse (as we haue sayde) by reason of the change of the ayre, often tymes chaunceth diuersitie and errour in the begynnynges of flowyng and reflowyng: For the violent disposition of wyndes, vehemently blowyng, as well neare, as farre of, rcmooueth the courses of waters from their due order, sometyme hastenyng the flowyng, and sometyme the reflowyng, and sometyme stayng or slackyng them lykewyse. *The influence of other Planettes, maye cause disorder in ebbyng and flowyng. And lykewyse vehement vvyndes.*

There

Of flowyng.

There chaunceth also errour in the mydst of motion of waters, for as wel courses of waters, as also flowynges and reflowynges, sometyme keepe not the due motion: For (as is sayd) the disposition of wyndes may either encrease or diminishe their courses. Furthermore also, the strapteнesse or narowneсse of places, by reason of Ilandes or mountaynes, cause great concourses and diuersities in many places. For where the sea is strayter or narower, there is the stronger course, as about the Iland Euboea, Nigropontis, and betweene Sicilia and Calabria is greatly obserued. Suche straytes hynder the encrease of waters, because lesse quantitie passeth thereby, and therefore there the flowynges and reflowynges are lesse. And hereupon it chaunceth, that in the Ocean sea, are greatest flowynges and reflowynges, because there are no straytes which may hynder or stay the courses of waters, and by that meanes they haue their full and free course, and in more certayne order. But in our sea, Mare Mediterraneum, it is otherwyse. For what so euer water of the Ocean entreth therein, or commeth foorth, passeth from the Weast by one onely narowe strayte: and therfore it can not in the flowyng be greatly fylled, neyther in the reflowyng be greatly emptied. And so consequently, the motion of the water of ỹ sea proceedeth not in certayne order. And to haue saide thus much of the diuers motions of the water of ỹ sea, may suffise.

Narowneсse of places may cause disorder.

A Demonstration of Proportions of *Motions Locall*, printed rather for the learned Philosopher, then the Mariner, yet the Mariner may learne many proper conclusions necessarie to be knowen.

To the godly and not enuious reader, Iohn Taisnier Hannonius, wisheth health, &c.

Hereas a fewe yeeres past, at *Rome*, *Ferraria*, and in other Vniuersities of *Italie* (when *Paul* the third possessed the *Papal* dignitie) I tooke in hande to reade publique lectures of sciences *Mathematike*, I may testifie without scruple of arrogancie, that my lectures were honourably accompanyed with the presence of more then three hundred auditors, because that artes *Mathematike* are there greatly esteemed. And therefore after the lecture was finished (as is the maner of auditors) oftentimes many resorted vnto me, departing frō the scholes, to demaund further of such doubtes, wherof they had not ful vnderstanding. In the meane while, certaine which enuied my reputation and assertions, ceassed not with iniuries, to hynder our proceedinges, and sometimes to make an ende of our disputations with quarrels and strokes. It chaunced in the meane tyme that mention was made of the lecture of *Aristotel*. And whereas, from the purpose, one enuious person moued the question of the *Proportions of Locall Motions*, I refused to dispute with hym, affirming that he euyll vnderstoode the intention of *Aristotel*, whom he so esteemed as a heauenly God, that it seemed to hym sacrilege, if any shoulde dissent from his doctrine. But he, malitiously and furiously, affirmed that I dyd rashly condemne *Aristotel*. I was therefore enforced by the

Demonstrations of Proportions, the request of my reuerende Cardinal of Adulphis Florentine, openly to repeate the same, especially for that the reporte of these contentions, was nowe come to the Popes eares, whose request also, I tooke for commaundement. And thereupon (whiche I had not doone before) I declared the errours of Aristotle, in the presence of the reuerende Cardinal Crescentius, and the Bishop of Ponset, men most expert in all kinde of learnyng, and in maner infinite other Auditours, before whom (in maner as foloweth) I shewed the errours of Aristotle by wordes and demonstrations. You therefore gentle and indifferent readers, accept this our Demonstration with fauourable myndes. I repute Aristotle for the chiefe of all Philosophers. Yet forasmuche as it is humane to erre, he also myght sometymes fayle.

Demonstration of the Proportions of Motions Locall, agaynst Aristotle and all Philosophers.

First of al, and before we shall touch the poynt of the Demonstration of Proportions of Motions locall, is to be noted, that of bodyes beyng of one and the same kinde, the like and self same is the proportion betwene quantities, whiche is also betweene heauinesse or lyghtnesse, eyther simply, or in respect to other, it maketh no matter. It is ynough, that among them whose proportion we shall consyder by quantitie, among the same lykewyse, we shall vnderstande by heauynesse and lyghtnesse. &c. Let be for example two bodyes of leade, and vnequall, as A. and E. of the which the body A. shalbe triple in quantitie to the body E. for of the multiplication of the body, let no man be deceiued: for many haue thought the sphere to be duplicate, when his Diameter is duplicate, whiche is a great errour, as appeareth by. 15. of the twelfth of Euclide. For there is shewed that the proportion of two spheres the one to the other, to be as it were the triplicate proportion of the Diameter of the greater sphere, to the Diameter of the lesse. Lykewise also is shewed in. 37. of the twelfth, of solid bodyes lyke, and equidistant superficies. Furthermore Albertus Durerus, speaketh sufficiently of this in his. 4. booke of Geometrie, teachyng the duplication of Cubus. &c. For then the same body A. shoulde exceede the body E. in heauynesse in triple proportion. Note therfore the weyght A. and the letter B. and E. be signed F. and conceiue in minde the body A. to be diuided into three equal parts, that is to say, C D G. of the which partes, H I K. nowe is it manifest for the presupposition, that euery part of, C D G. in equallitie shal correspond to ye body E. and shal waygh by common science, equally F. which yf it were not

Albertus Durerus.

Cubus is a square figure lyke a Dye.

D ii

Demonstrations of Proportions,

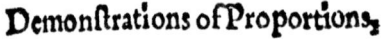

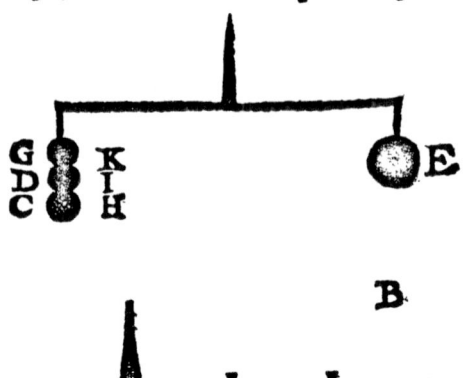

not, euery part of A. shoulde not be reputed Homogenie, or all of one lyke substance with the body E. and so shoulde it repugne with the presupposed. Therfore, forasmuch as H I K. togeather is equiualent to B. only by common science, shalbe also (by the 7. of the fyfth) B. to F. the same that is H I K. to the same F. but the weyght of H I K. is triple to F. by whiche reason the proposition is manifest.

I wyll nowe make Demonstration howe bodyes of the selfe same, or one kinde and figure, equall or vnequal one to the other, in the same middest or meane, by equall space, be moued in one or selfe same time: the which is agaynst Aristotel and all other philosophers that haue not yet seene this proposition. Aristotel first in the 4. of his phisickes, Cap. De Vacuo, where he intendeth to shewe, that yf Vacuum, or voyde, be graunted, mouyng or motion is taken away, &c. he there sayth thus, We see those bodyes whiche haue more heauynesse or lyghtnesse, so that they be of one figure, to be more swyftly moued by equal space, and by such proportion as they haue the one to the other. And therefore they are so moued, per Vacuum. &c. which is proued to be false. Furthermore what S. Thomas sayth touchyng this, any man that wil, may reade: for no man euer better vnderstood y minde

Thomas de Aquino.

of

of Motions Locall.

of Aristotle. But for the examples which Simplicius and Auerroes geue to the vnderstandyng of this (by two sphericall bodyes of equal quantitie, but of diuers kindes, as one of gold, & the other of syluer) we must not therfore say that they vnderstood this proposition as I wyll demonstrate. For they shoulde haue sayde somewhat of the equalitie of the quantitie of these bodyes, forasmuche as the motion of bodyes equall or vnequall, is all one, so that they be all of one figure: as for example, yf there be three spherical bodyes, of the which two be of gold, and the thyrd of syluer, and they of golde be vnequall, and the other of syluer equal to one of the golden bodyes: then in the same proportion of tyme, shalbe moued the golden body equall to that of syluer, with the syluer body, in the whiche proportion the syluer body with the golden vnequall, as shalbe declared hereafter. *Motiõ of the bodies of gold and siluer.*

Furthermore 6. Phisicorum. Cap. 1. in the ende, and in maner through al the. 2. Chapter of the same booke, he confirmeth the same: but in the fourth he sayth thus, Whereas euery thyng that moueth, moueth in some other, & in some time, and that moueable is motion of the whole, the same or all one shalbe the diuisions of the tyme and the mouyng, and of to be moued, and of that which is moued, and also of that in the whiche is mouyng. Afterward he geueth demonstration after his maner: but cap. 7. he wylleth the same, where he intendeth, that in finite tyme, nothyng may passe into infinite greatnesse. &c. Furthermore Aristotle in his fyrst booke, De Cœlo, confirmeth the same, saying simply that the reason or consyderation of tymes, is contrary to the reason of weyghtes: as yf halfe a weight be moued in this time, the double is moued in the halfe of this. &c. And this cap. 6. Furthermore cap. 8. of the same booke he sayth, The fire in as muche as it is greater then the earth, so muche the sooner and swyftlyer it commeth to his restyng place. &c. *The motion of fyre.*

Also in his seconde booke, De Cœlo. Cap. 8. he sayth thus: As in other things, the greater body, is more swyftly moued by his proper course or motion, euen so also in the heauenly circles, &c. Agayne Cap. 13. he affirmeth the same in two places, saying that the greater earth, is euer swyftlyer moued. *Motion of heauenly circles.*

Item, lib. De Cœlo cap. 2. he sayth thus, If accordyng to

D iii the

Demonstration of Proportions,

the proportion whiche hath the space C D. the body of B. shalbe diuided, all B. in the same tyme shalbe moued by C E. in thy whiche tyme parte of B. by C D. of necessitie: wherefore it foloweth that B. be moued with swyfter motion then parte of B. Afterwarde he maketh lyke Demonstration, saying thus, The swyftnesse of the lesse, to the swyftnesse of the greater, hath suche proportion as the greater bodye to the lesse, &c. Agayne in the thyrde, De Cœlo. Cap. 5. in the ende he sayth lykewyse, that so muche the more euery thyng is moued, as it is the greater, as also the fire the greater it is, is so muche of swyfter motion, &c. He confirmeth the same also, Cap. 2. and 4. of the same booke, where yet speakyng more clearely, he sayth that the greater fire ryseth vpwarde swyfter then a lesse: and a greater peece of gold or leade, doth swyfter moue downewarde, and the lyke of other heauy bodyes: and more clearely can no man geather the meanyng of Aristotle.

Vitellio, in his seconde booke of Perspectiue in the seconde proposition, hath fallen into the same errour. I pretermit his ignorance in that proposition where he thynketh that there is no quantitie insensible: but let this passe with other errours, the whiche at any other tyme shalbe shewed in theyr place. He that wyll reade all other Philosophers, shall see that they all accorde with the mynde and sentence of Aristotle, who also in diuers other places confirmeth the same: but to haue rehearsed these principall places, may suffise, and therefore we wyll nowe come to the Demonstration.

This propounded Demonstration, I wyll shew apparently, that it may the better be vnderstoode. And forasmuche, as Archimedes in his woorke, De insidentibus quæ, hath spoken nothyng of the proportion of motion of Elementes, it is manifest that he had not yet searched this proposition: for there was the proper place of this matter. But it is not graunted to any one man to knowe all thynges: and therefore it was very difficult to many to imagine the supposition, whiche I openly expounded in Rome, whereas Archimedes maketh none other Demonstration, but that naturall motion is not caused of any other then of the excesse or proceedyng of a bodye in an Element.

The greater body the quicker motion.

The greater fire the swyfter motion.

Perspectiue & errour of Vitellio.

Archimedes.

of Motions Locall.

ment, aboue or vpon the sayde Element, or contrarywyse. &c.

Demonstration.

LEt be for example two bodyes, G. and D. both alyke, that is to meane, spherical and Homogenie (that is) altogeather of lyke substaunce: of the which D. shal exceede G. in quadruple proportion (for yf it shall exceede it in quantitie, it shall also exceede in heauynesse as it is sayde before) and that the meane or myddle be vniforme, as B D F M V. For example: let the termining lynes be equidistant, and the same also circular vpon the centre S. Then by the terminyng lyne, from whence, let passe, or be drawne the lyne. P I Q. and by the terminyng lyne to whom, let passe the lyne R M V T. Thus I conclude, the bodyes G. and D. to be moued in vnequall tyme by the sayde space, by the motion of nature in the aforesayde meane: but yf the body D. were equall to the body G. there were no doubt, but that those bodyes shoulde be moued in equall tyme by the same space. &c. I wyll therefore by imagination diuide the body D. into foure equall partes, lyke vnto their whole. Let be therfore those partes signified by the letters, H K L N. whose centers (for example) I wyll put in the lyne P Q. so that the distance betweene H. and K. be the same that is betweene L. and N. I wyll also diuide the lyne K L. by equalitie, by the 29. of the thyrde of Euclides in the poynt I. whiche shalbe the centre of the heauynesse of the bodyes H K. and L N. by common science mainteyned, by the third propositiō of the booke of Archimedes, De centris grauium. Furthermore it is manifest, that euery one of the bodyes, H K L N. shalbe moued in equall tyme from the terminyng lyne or space of P I Q. to the terminyng lyne R V M T. to that in the whiche is G. By the fyrst conception therefore of Euclides, all bodyes, that is to meane H K L N. and G. passyng togeather from and at the same instant, shalbe moued

A quo
Ad quem.

D iiii equally,

Demonstration of Proportions,

equally, that is to say, in equall tyme: and euer the lyne passyng by their centres, shalbe equally distant to the lyne R M U T. Finally yf the lyne be vnderstoode by the centre I. and the body D. diuided by equalitie or equall distance, then that poynt of diuision, shalbe the centre of the weyght H K L N. and D. by the aforesayde. But nowe if that lyne be vnderstoode to be moued by force of the foresayde bodyes, and demissed from the lyne P Q. or equidistant to it (for the also should M U R T. be equidistant) by common sense, M U R T & the body D. in equall tyme by the motion of nature shalbe moued by the grater space, to that in the which the bodyes H K L N. shalbe moued: For resistaunce of the meane to the bodyes H K L N. is the same whiche is to the body D. But that this may appeare more manifest, let it be thus vnderstoode. Let vs imagine (for example) two bodyes of water: Of the whiche, the one shalbe equall in quantitie to the body D and the other to the body G. or to one of the bodyes N L K H. whiche shalbe all one: then 16. of the fyfth, the proportion of D. to G. or to one of the aforesayde bodyes, is the same which is of the waterie equall D. to the waterie equall G. by the proposition declared before:

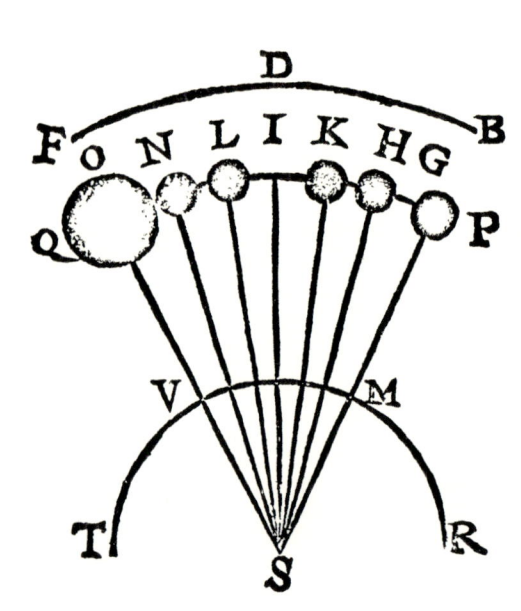

Proportion and motion of waterie bodyes.

Th

of Motions Local.

The proportion of heauynesse of the watrie body equall C to the heauynesse of the watrie body equall G. is the same whiche is betweene the quantities of the selfe same bodyes: But we must vnderstande them to be susteyned or weyghed in a rarer or thynner Element. The proportion therefore shalbe the same which is betwene the heauynesse of bodyes D. and G. by the. 11. of the fyfth, the aforesayd proposition helpyng thereto. Furthermore, let vs imagine the heauynesse of watrie bodyes, to be substract from the heauines of the bodyes, D. and G. So the other grauities or heauynesse, shalbe those whiche shalbe mooued without impediment, as appeareth by the 7. of Archimedes, De insidentibus aquæ.

And whereas by the 15. of the fyfth of Euclides, the proportion of these heauie bodyes, is the same which is betweene D. and G. by the. 19. of the fyfth aforesayd: the resystaunce of the meane or myddle to D. shalbe quadruple to the resystance to G. The same also doo I say of euery of the bodyes N L K H. It appeareth by common science, that resystance of the meane to the bodyes N L K H. is equal to that whiche is to the body D. but is the same in the which G. by the fyrst conception of Euclides.

Furthermore, yf there shalbe two bodyes of al one fygure, but of diuers homogeneite or substance, and of vnequall corporalitie, and (for example) either of them heauier then the meane or myddle, in the which they are mooued, and that also the lesse of them be heauier then the bigger, yet that the greater weygh more then the lesse, then I say, that the lesse shalbe swyfter in motion: and the same shalbe the proportion of tyme to the lesse, whiche is to the greater, which is also the greater kynde of heauynesse to the kynde of ye lesse, takyng away so much heauines from both, as is of the halfe in euery of them. Let be for example, two bodies M. and N. of the same fourme, & diuers homogeneite or substance, and the same also to be vnequal (for of equals there is no doubt) of the which, the greater shalbe M but the kynde of the body N. to be heauier then the kynde of the body M. Puttyng the case also, that the body M. be heauier then the body N. & each of them also heauier then the meane or myddle body, by the whiche they mooue: then wyll I shewe the proposition. Vnderstande fyrste

I V I.

Demonstrations of Proportions

A U I. to be of equall and lyke fygure to the body M. but of the kynde of the body N. Let vs imagine also that the body M. in heauynesse, to exceede the myddle or meane in double proportion A U I. or in the eyght proportion: so then the moouyng of the body A U I. shall in the seuenth proportion be swyfter then the motion of the body M. becauſe the reſyſtance of the halfe to the body M. is ſubdupla, & to the body A U I. ſuboctupla, by the ſeuenth of Archimedes, De inſidentibus aquæ. But by the aforeſayd Demonſtration, the body N. ſhalbe moued in the ſame tyme in whiche the body A U I. Wherefore, by the fyrſte conception of the minde added vppon Euclide by Campanus, the propoſition is cleare.

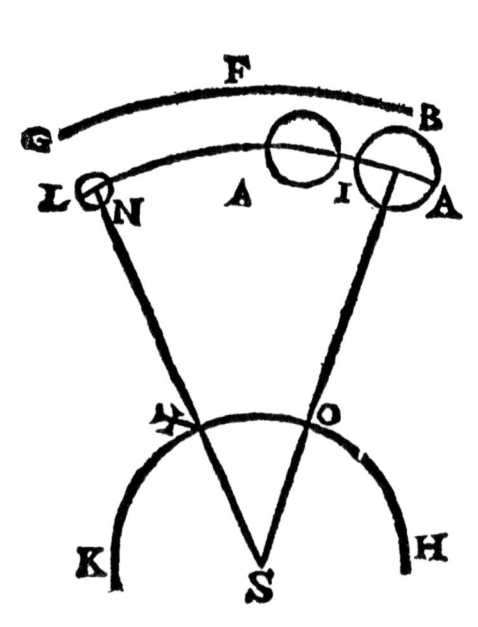

Motions violent and naturall.

The lyke reaſon is alſo of violent motions, takyng the proportion of the moouyng ſtrengthes, and takyng away the proportion of the reſyſtaunce of the halfe or myddle. Alſo, whereas are two equall angles aboue the Horizon, or vnder, but in contrary order to the motion of nature, becauſe violent motion is ſwyfter in the begynnyng then in the ende: and the contrary ſhall in-

of Motions Local.

chaunceth in the motion of nature: For with violent motion, the motion of nature is euer somewhat myxt, yf horizontally or angulerly it shalbe aboue or beneathe the Horizon: and nature woorketh so much, untyl it bryng violent motion vnto some ende. But yf perpendiculerlye violence shalbe made aboue the Horizon, and towarde the place whiche that body naturally mooueth vnto, then nature can not stryue agaynst or withstande, but that violence doeth euer goe with it, in respecte of the ende from whence. Furthermore, by the afore sayde, it is manyfest that to be false whiche Aristotle sayth 7. Physic. in the last chapter, where he sayth, Yf A. be that whiche mooueth B. and B. that whiche is mooued, and C. the longitude whereby, and D. the tyme in whiche the motion is, that is to say, in equall tyme and power equall. A. the halfe of B. shall mooue by the double of C. and by C. in the halfe of D. for so shalbe the similitude of the reason. &c. That it is false I wyll thus demonstrate. Let vs fyrst imagine two bodyes as before, in any meane or myddle homogenie. &c. As let be for example. M. and N. and that M. be double in quantitie to the body N. and that the weyght of N. be al one with the weyght of M. And also that the body A U I. be equal to the body M. in quantitie, & in lykenesse or kynde of the body N. Then by common science, the body A U I. shalbe double in heauynesse to the body M. And grauntyng that the body M. be double in heauynesse aboue the halfe, then shall the body A U I. be quadruple in heauynesse aboue the sayde halfe. Wherefore the resystance taken away, let be left the tyme in the whiche the body A U I. to the tyme in the whiche M. is in proportion subtriple, or in the whiche the body A U I. in the same tyme shalbe mooued the body N. by the aforesayd. Or yf in the same tyme the body N. shalbe mooued with the bodye M. yet the space by the whiche N. shalbe triple to that by whiche M. For the reason is all one of violent motions. The same shall precisely come to passe, yf in the steade of the excesse of weyght aboue the halfe, we shal take the vertue or power moouyng. &c. as before.

Aristotle

Demonstrations of Proportions

Aristotle lykewyse erreth in 4.Physic. Cap.8. where he entreateth De vacuo, sayinge that the same, or al one, shalbe the proportion of motions of any body by diuers Elementes, which is betweene the same Elementes. As yf the ayre be in subtilitie double to the water, in double tyme B. the meane shall passe to that tyme, in whiche by the meane D. and C. the tyme shalbe double of the tyme E. &c. Nowe I shewe the errour of Aristotle. Let vs fyrste vnderstande, a body to passe through water by natural motion, as (for example) by a graunted space,

The proportion of motion of Elementes.

let vs also imagine that body in double to exceede the water in weyght, and that the water in heauynesse exceede the ayre in double proportion, then the graunted body shalbe quadruple to the ayre. Wherfore in the heauynesse, the resystences of tyme taken away, in the whiche the motion of that body in the ayre, by equall space to that, by the whiche in water to the tyme wherein by water in the graunted space is moued, the proportion shalbe subtriple, and not subduple, as Aristotle affyrmeth. Aristotle also erreth in the same Chapter, supposyng that yf motion shoulde be graunted in voyde, the same or all one, shoulde be the reason of tyme to tyme, as is betwene moouyng bodyes: whiche is impossible by the aforesayde. For those bodyes shoulde be moued in equall tyme, although they shoulde be of diuers kyndes, fourmes, and bygnesse. By which place also is easye to gather, that the mynde of Aristotle was, that the proportion of motion to motion, is the same whiche greatnesses haue betweene them, accordyng to heauynesse and lyghtnesse simply. But that this also maye be more clearely vnderstoode, imagine the bodyes M. and N. in voyde, and that the body N. be of the same weyght whiche A U I. but of diuers kyndes, and consequently, of diuers bygnesse: then whereas those bodyes haue no resystence, there is no doubt but they shalbe moued in equal tyme, by equal space. I wyl take therfore the body A U I. of the kynde of the body N. but of the quantitie of the body M. nowe then by the meane of true methode of the demonstration before shewed A U I. & N. shalbe moued in equall tyme with the body N. by equal space. Wherefore, by the fyrste conception in the same in the which M: wherfore it foloweth. &c.

Fur-

of Motions Local.

Furthermore, also where Aristotle. 7. Physic. speaketh of the comparison of motions, saying that a ryght lyne is not comparable to a crooked lyne, because there should be found some ryght lyne equal of circuler lyne, eyther greater or lesse. For whereas by reason of the definition geuen by him in 6. Physic. to the swyftnesse and slownesse of motion, it seemeth to him that it can not be, that circuler motion shoulde be comparable to ryght motion. In the which he is manyfestly deceyued, & cheefely, thynkyng that a ryght lyne can not be founde equall, greater or lesser to the circuler lyne: whereas Archimedes in the fyrst propositiō of his Geometrie, sheweth the contrary, and that by Mathematicall demonstration, and not by the opinion of Aristotle. For Archimedes sheweth there, by what meanes we may finde a ryght lyne greater or lesse then any circuler lyne, constitutyng fygures of right lynes without or within the circle. &c. But some man may say, that although a ryght lyne may be graunted greater or lesse then anye circuler lyne, yet that the same can not be founde equal, whereas in.15.of the thyrde of Euclide, is shewed

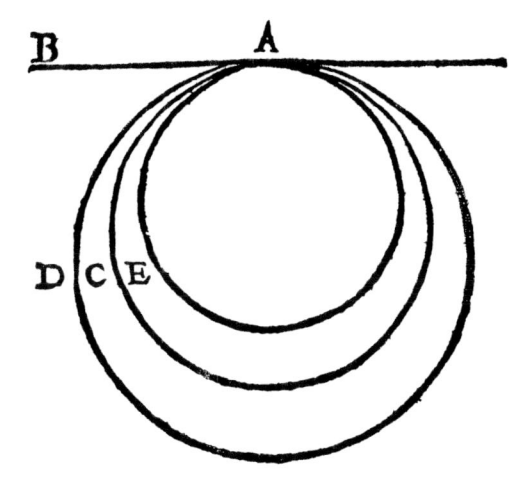

that a greater Angle may be founde, then is the angle of Contingence, and that by the motion of the ryght lyne of the greater angle,

Demonstrations of Proportions,

gle, passage is made vnto the ryght lyne contingent or touchyng the circle: Yet that it can not be, that with the contingent lyne it shoulde make an angle equall to the angle of contingence. To this I answeare, that although a greater angle be graunted, yet not a lesse: For yf the lesse shoulde be graunted as well as the greater, we shoulde lykewyse haue an equall. For example, consyder the circle A C. with the lyne A B. dooth touche in the poynt A. the angle of contingence shalbe A B C. then let be the circle inwardlye described A E. touchyng the circle A C. in the poynt A. for to one onely poynt it shall touche the circle A C. by 12. of the thyrde. And so the lyne A B. shall touche the circle A E by common science, by the which the angle B A E. shoulde be greater then the angle B A C. Lykewyse also, yf the circle A D. shalbe described outwardlye, the angle B A D. shoulde be lesse then the angle B A C. And consequently by the same order whereby we make the greater or the lesse, we shal also constitute equall, whiche is the intent.

Wherefore it foloweth, that it may be done contrary to that whiche Aristotle sayth, and for the same sentence of Aristotle, some haue thought that it is impossible that anye of the fygures of crooked lynes, shoulde be founde equal to any fygure of ryght lyne, or the contrary. The which to be possible, I wyll nowe demonstrate. For example, let be geuen a trigon or triangle A B C. for that I say of the trigon, I meane also of all fygures of ryght lynes, for as muche as they be diuisible into triangles, as appeareth by the 32 of the fyrst. And yf of those triangles we shal constitute a superficiall lyne of equidistant sydes, by 44. of the fyrste, taken as often as neede shalbe, whiche duplicate by the helpe of 36. of the fyrste, and afterwarde a Diameter in it, then the halfe of that superficies, shall haue an equall triangle of the taken superficies by the 41. of the fyrste, or by the taken ryght lyne by the fyrste conception, I wyll constitute a superficiall of two crooked lynes conteyned equall vnto it. I wyll diuide the fyrste Basis or grounde A C. by equall spaces into poyntes H. by 10 of the fyrste, and I drawe B H. whiche also I drawe foorth vntyll H K. be double to B H. by 3. of the fyrste twyse assumpted. Then to the halfe

of

of H R. that is I. I direct C I. and A I. I ioyne thereto also
A K. and C K. by ryght lynes: then (by the fyrst of the syxth)
these triangles shalbe all equall to them selues. After this,
I wyll constitute a superficiall of equidistant sydes, and of
ryght angles vppon what so euer lyne, whiche superficies
shalbe equall to the Poligonie A B C K. by 44 of the fyrst
assumpted, as often as shalbe needefull, that superficies
is made G D. But in the whiche I drawe the Diameter
F E. so that by 41. of the fyrst trigon F G E. shalbe the
halfe of the whole superficies, and by common science equal
to the trigon B K C. and triplus to the trigon B H C. nowe
I diuide F G. by equall in the poynt M. by 10 of the fyrst,
and I protracte or drawe foorth equidistantly G E. by 31. of
the fyrst. So doo I also of the lyne M L. diuiding it by equal
in the poynt N. by the aforesayde 10. of the fyrst. Afterwarde
by 44. of the fyrst twyse assumpted of equidistaunt sydes, I
make a superficies of ryght angles vpon the lyne M N. equal
to the quadrature of the lyne F M. which may consyst of M N.
and N D. Furthermore, of M N. transuerse or ouerthwarte,
and N D. ryght, I constitute a parabol of a ryght angle, that
it may be of lesse labour: For this example may suffice by 52. of
the fyrst of Apolonius Pergeus, the terminyng lyne of which *Apollonius*
paraboll, shall passe by the poyntes F N. and G. by the same, *Pergeus.*
and by 33. of the same F E. shal touch the parabol at the poynt
F. And afterwarde when the trigon F E G. shalbe triplus,
to the trigon B H C. as we haue shewed before, but also
the portion F N G. triplus by the 17. of Archimedes, De
quadratura Parabolæ. Wherefore the portion F N G. shalbe equall to the trigon H B C. by the fyrst conception in
Euclide, added by Campanus. Furthermore, I drawe E G.
vntyll by the thyrde of the fyrst G R. equall G R. I drawe
foorth also F R. and L M D: Then by the fourth of the fyrst,
the triangle F G E. shalbe of equall sydes, and also of equall
angles to the triangle F G R. Furthermore, Q M is equidistant G R. by common science, & by R G. of the fyrst, the angle
F Q M. equal to the angle F R G and the angle F R G equal
to the angle F M Q. and wheras the angle F R G is comon to
eyther

Demonſtrations of Proportions,

eyther of them, then by the 4. of the ſyxt, the ſame, or al one, ſhalbe the proportion R G. to Q M. as is of G F. to M F. But as is G F. to M F. ſo is G F. to M L. Wherefore by N. of the fift, G F. ſo hath it ſelfe to M L. as G R. to Q M. But by the 16. of the ſame M L. to Q M. hath it ſelfe, as G F. to G R. Wherefore M L. equall. M Q. whiche M Q. I diuide by equall in the poynt E by 10. of the fyrſt, & wyl doo as before. Then by the reaſons aforeſayde of the ſame, the portion F E G ſhalbe equall to the trigon A B H. and the whole Superficies F G. N E. ſhalbe equall to the whole trigon, A B C. whiche is propoſed.

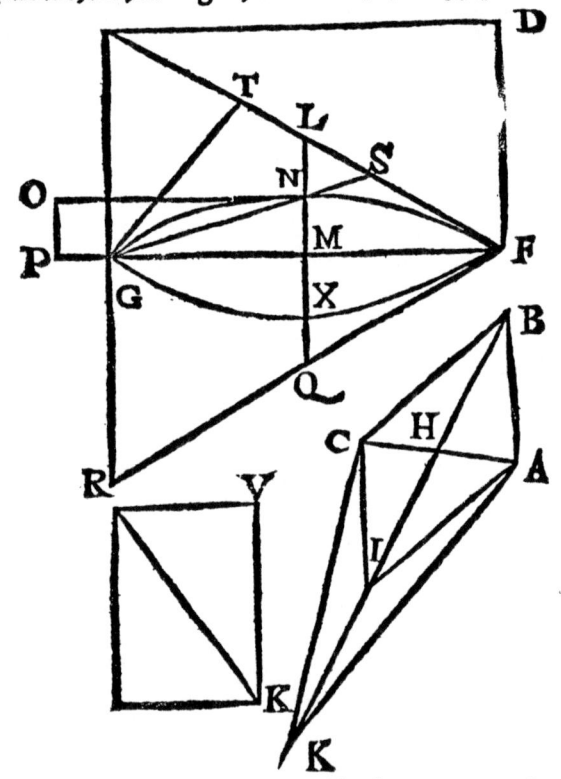

The contrary appeareth thus. Let be graunted a Superficies, conteyned of two paraboll lynes, as F N G. and F E G.
pro.

of Motions Locall.

proposing (for example) to fynde a superficiall of ryght lynes trianguler equal to the graunted superficies. I drawe fyrst F G. Then after by 44. of the second of Apollonius Pergeus, I find the Diameter of the parabol F N G. whiche is M N. whiche I draw to N L. to be equall M N. Then I drawe F L. which shal touch the parabol F N G. in the poynt F. by 33. of the first of the same. Then from the poynt G. I draw a lyne G E. equidistant fro the Diameter M N L. by 31. of the fyrst of Euclide: whiche I drawe vntyll it iopne togeather with F L. the whiche doubtlesse shalbe done by the second of the first of Vitellio.

The poynt of the concourse or ioyning togeather, is E. then I diuide F E. into three equal portions by the 11. of the syxth of Euclide, in the poyntes S. and T. which poyntes I iopne with the poynt G. by the lynes F G. and G R. Nowe shall there be three angles all equall to them selues by 38. of Euclide. After this, I constitute a Trigon, B H C. equall to the Trigon, F S G. by this meanes I drawe foorth H C. to the equalitie G S. by the 4. of the first of Euclide. Then at the poynt H. I designe an angle B H C. equall to the angle F S G. by 23. of the first of Euclide: and by 3. of the first of the same, I drawe H B. vntyl it be equall F S. Afterwarde I ioyne B C. by a lyne. Then by 4. of the first, the tryangle B H C. shalbe equall to the triangle F S G. and shalbe equal to the portion F N G. by 17. Archimedes, De Quadratura parabolæ, by the helpe of the first conception of Euclide. I do the like of the portion F G E. to whom by an equall triangle D P K. Then I drawe P Q equally distant D K. and K U. equally distant D P. by 31. of the first of Euclide. Then by 41. of the same D P K. shalbe halfe of the superficies D U. Now then I somwhat protract C H. then vpon B H. I constitute a superficiall of equidistant sides, hauyng an angle B H A. by 44. of the first of Euclide, twyse assumpted: the Diameter of the which superficies, be A P B. Then by 41. of the same with the first conception of the Trigon A B C. shalbe equal of the superficies F G N E. graunted, which is the intent.

Aristotle (to say the trueth) was an excellent searcher of *Aristotle.* things: Yet I wyl not say as some say (which haue neuer read ye workes of Aristotle, or vnderstande thē not) that euery word of

E t Aristotle

Demonstrations of Proportions,

Aristotle, is almost a sentence: & that Aristotle was the god of Philosophers, & neuer erred in one worde, but was diuine in all things. Such miserable men, if they knew what it were to speake with Demonstration, & what by experience to the sense, woulde neuer haue said such thyngs. For by sense simply, in those things that are not properly sensible, we are oftentymes deceiued. And wheras we can not perceiue the deception, by the meane of that simple sense, then it semeth to vs that the thing can not be, & that it is not in very deede as it appeareth to the sense, as for example: Who is he that thinkyng not a reflexed forme on the superficiall of water immoueable, to be seene of the same greatnesse, as it is by a ryght longitude, by the meane of a Diaphane, geathered of a radiall lyne incident and reflecte: wheras this is false by G Q of the sixth of Vitellio. For the superficies of the water is sphericall, as sheweth Aristotle. 2. De Cœlo. Cap. 4. But better Archimedes in the 2. proposition, De subsidentibus aquæ. And therfore when any starre appeareth vnto vs aboue the Horizon, yet is it not in deede as it appeareth: but is rather vnder the Horizon, as appeareth by this Demonstration. Let the starre be I. the Horizon R A T. the earth E A M. whose center

The sense indgeth not truely of all thynges sensible.

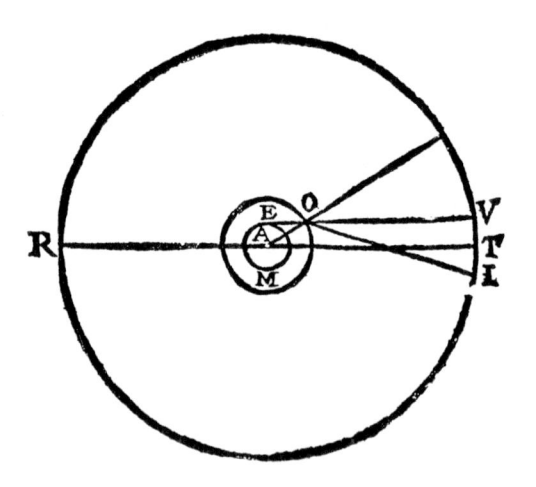

is A. & the sight E. the vapours D E. Then whereas the radiall lyne

of Motions Local.

lyne passyng from any rare, thynne, or transparent in anye transparent of more thycknesse, maketh a perpendiculer, by the 45 of the seconde of Vitellio, it is manyfest therefore the starre I. to be seene by the lyne I D E. which lyne shalbe crooked, because that simple ayre is thynner then vapours, and fyre thynner then ayre. Also the matter or substance of heauen is thynner then fyre, by 50 of the 10. of Vitellio. Furthermore, the hygher parte of the ayre is thynner then the lower parte. The same I say also of water and fyre (yf we may cal fyre the hyghest part of the body, neare vnto the concauitie of the Moone) and of euery superior part of Elementes. And so the starre by the lyne D E. seemeth to be aboue the Horizon, in the poynt U. But Vitellio also in the tenth booke, in the proposition 49. teacheth perspetiuely, and howe it may be instrumentally prooued, howe the starres maye be seene in the Horizon, without their proper places, by reason of incuruation or crookyng of the beames. Wherof it foloweth, that they doo not Mathematically define the Horizon, which say that it is the terminer or ender of the syght, and of the greatest circles of the Sphere, wheras by the demonstrations before, the circle endyng the syght, is cuttyng the Sphere in two vnequall portions, and that the hygher portion be greater then the lower. For yf the Horizon be the ender of the syght, and one of the greatest circles, then the earth is not equally about the centre or middle of the worlde, or els the myddle of the worlde is without the earth. But yf the earth doeth equally compasse about the myddle, ergo the ender of the syght is not of the greatest circles in the Sphere, or contrarylp. Therefore yf we shal see any starre aboue the ender of the syght, we shoulde not therefore thynke it to be in the twelfth station of heauen (this is to be vnderstood by reasonable maner) for the vertue of the starre appeareth cheefly in the great circle (whose Pole is Zenith) passyng by the 90. degree of the Equinoctial, from the intersection or diuidyng of the same with the Meridian toward the East. Furthermore, the difference betweene the ender of the syght and the greater circle, is not of onely one Diameter of the starre, but of degrees, whiche yf it were not, we coulde by no meanes vse the proposition 49. of Vitellio: And therefore it was no small errour of them that

The thynnesse and thycknesse of Elementes.

The true and false definition of the Horizon.

sayd

Demonstrations of Proportions,
sayde that the Horizon is the ender of the syght, and one of the greatest circles in the Sphere, & that euer the myddle of heauen appeareth vnto vs, for euermore the halfe appeareth vnto vs: for the incuruation or crookyng of the beames. But he that wyl see more examples of these thynges, let hym reade the fourth booke of Vitellio, and the tenth, and somewhere the seconde and fyfth of the same. In euery of them he shal see somewhat howe easyly we may be deceyued by this sense: and the lyke of other senses is not to be doubted. Therfore not without weake & slender iudgement, they call Aristotle so diuine a Prince of Philosophie, as though he could not erre. And therfore that excellent Philosopher, and Diuine, Peter Arches, dyd very wysely geue commendation and honour to Aristotle proportionally, and no further, but onely to God: To whom be all honour and glorie. So be it.

Proportion in comendation.

FINIS.